mary corpening barber and sara corpening whiteford

WITH LORI LYN NARLOCK

cocktail
FOOD

50 finger foods *with attitude*

PHOTOGRAPHS BY *carin krasner*

CHRONICLE BOOKS

SAN FRANCISCO

acknowledgments

This cookbook is a compilation of insight, talent, and unwavering support from some very special people. Our most sincere thanks to:

Patricia Willets, who pulled us through at every turn and provided magnificent culinary vision and tremendous decision-making ability.

Bill LeBlond, our editor, for his vision and, more importantly, for his heartfelt advice.

Jane Dystel, our savvy agent, for her perseverance and guidance.

Jack and Erik, our husbands, for being the most honest recipe testers in the world and for being patient when we were working around the clock and not available.

Jackson, our newest addition, who has provided inspiration to both of us during the tedious testing process.

Mom and Dad, our guiding lights, for their undying support.

Tori Ritchie, for being our number one mentor.

Sara Deseran, for listening and for her sound advice.

Various friends and recipe testers, especially to Victoria Reid, Lucy Bowen Caddell, Bruce Taylor, Gerri Shaw, Liza Williams, Larry Kandell, Wayne Hill, Andrea Cardoso, Tania and Richard Bennett, Mandy Schoch, Jeff Licata, Libit Schoch, Ann Beattie, Bill Whiteford, Mary Adkins, Lauren Bruder, and last but not least, Franck Prissert.

—*Mary and Sara*

Library of Congress Cataloging-in-Publication Data:
Barber, Mary Corpening, 1969–
    Cocktail Food : 50 finger foods with attitude/ by Mary Corpening Barber and Sara Corpening Whiteford, with Lori Lyn Narlock; photographs by Carin Krasner.
    p. cm.
    Includes index.
    ISBN 0-8118-2418-7 (hc.)
    1. Appetizers. 2. Cocktail parties. 3 Entertaining.
    I. Whiteford Corpening, Sara, 1969–
    II. Narlock, Lori Lyn, 1962– III. Title.
    TX740.B37   1999
    641.8'12—dc21
                            98-55736
                            CIP

Printed in Hong Kong.

Food styling by Kimberly Huson
Prop styling by Kim Wong
Photography assistant Eric Staudenmaier
The photographer wishes to thank Julia Flagg, Tricia Burlingham, and Carolyn Garris.

Designed by CAROLE GOODMAN/BLUE ANCHOR DESIGN

Distributed in Canada by Raincoast Books
8680 Cambie Street
Vancouver, British Columbia V6P 6M9

10 9 8 7 6 5 4 3 2

Chronicle Books
85 Second Street
San Francisco, California 94105

www.chroniclebooks.com

table of contents

53 not too strong, not too weak

WELL-BALANCED HORS D'OEUVRES
THAT COMPLEMENT A RANGE OF
BEVERAGES, FROM DAIQUIRIS TO
GIN AND TONICS

94 light and delicate

introduction

IF YOU'VE HAD ONE TOO MANY CHIPS FROM A BAG, DIPS FROM A JAR, OR carrot sticks, you and your friends will be refreshed, bite after bite, with *Cocktail Food*. This book is filled with innovative recipes for scrumptious, sexy, doable finger food.

We have been hosting parties for as long as we can remember—helping our parents as children, throwing our own parties as teenagers, and catering professionally for the majority of our culinary careers. After preparing and serving an endless array of delicious finger foods, we chose fifty of our favorite combinations for this book. They redefine party food by capturing global flavors in bite-sized treats.

We have always had a passion for sharing recipes and entertaining tips. Our enthusiasm has grown as a result of hours of conversation with people asking for advice and recipes. We have filled this book with the information that our friends and clients frequently request and we hope that it will inspire and boost the confidence of any host with cocktail-party jitters.

In *Cocktail Food* we provide contemporary recipes that are simple yet stylish. We have included do-ahead tips for every recipe to accommodate the reality of everyone's fast-paced life.

The recipes are divided into chapters based on the flavor intensity of the ingredients so that they will complement a potable's potency. But that doesn't mean you can't mix and match, or leave out the drinks altogether and simply indulge in a savory little snack.

If you love a good party as much as we do, open this book and start cooking up your next cocktail party!

cocktail-party basics

Do you want to jump-start a relationship? Entertain future in-laws? Make amends with a neighbor? Pour them a drink, give them something to snack on, and stand back. A libation and an accompanying morsel are all that is needed to make up the most revered of occasions: a cocktail party.

A cocktail party is an ideal form of entertaining because it can be a limited investment of time. It doesn't require toiling over a six-course menu, dusting off that full set of china, or running out of dessert forks. A cocktail party can be a planned occasion or an impromptu gathering. It can be elaborate or simple, it's all up to you. There are no rules for throwing a great soiree, other than relaxing and having fun. After all, it's your party.

We do have a few suggestions to get you started on your next party. Make a plan and stick to your guns; stock up on both food and drinks (more is always better); present your offerings attractively; and pair the food and drinks to complement, not overwhelm, each other.

make a plan

Whether you are sending out invitations to an occasion weeks in advance or inviting friends over at the last minute, make a game plan. Start with lists. Write down how many people are invited and the intended party length. Be realistic; remember that these types of gatherings do have a tendency to run overtime and over budget. Next, decide what food and drinks you want to serve. Do your budget and menu jibe? Be careful not to plan a champagne extravaganza when your wallet is screaming beer bash.

Do you have time to execute your desired plan? Don't be overambitious or unrealistic. It's OK to serve a limited selection. Wow guests with one or two special hors d'oeuvres paired with one type of liquor rather than making yourself crazy with a large selection. Consider your schedule and then make a time-line. Write down everything that can be accomplished ahead of time and a separate list to keep track of everything that needs to be tackled at the last minute. Plan to buy liquor in advance and perishables the day of the party. Then match these lists with your calendar and, if possible, spread tasks evenly so that you aren't burdened on any one day. Schedule baking and cooking items that can be frozen first; next, plan for items that can be prepared and refrigerated or left at room temperature; finish with items that require last-minute assembly.

The most important aspect of selecting your menu is to consider how much preparation time is needed for each recipe. Vary your menu so that not all of the dishes need to be heated and/or assembled at the last minute. Select one or two recipes that can be completed ahead of time and served cold or at room temperature. Mix in one or two dishes that are served with a minimum of last-minute fanfare. Add one or two warm dishes that can be passed. Also keep in mind who your guests will be. Are you entertaining your husband's sports buddies or your mother's garden club?

the numbers game

Whether your cocktail party is an event unto itself or a prelude to a later meal, the secret to success is always stocking more than you think you need. It's always hospitable to offer a few less labor-intensive items, such as a cheese and fruit platter or pâté with crackers. You'll have peace of mind and your guests will definitely be satiated.

If your cocktail party is the main event and not just to whet your guests' appetites for dinner, plan for 5 hors d'oeuvres per hour per person for the first 2 hours and 3 hors d'oeuvres per person each hour afterward. For example, if you are hosting 8 people for 2 hours, prepare 80 pieces of food. You can double and triple recipes to yield your targeted number of hors d'oeuvres. If your party will be followed by a meal, reduce the number of hors d'oeuvres to about 4 per hour per person.

Pick your potion and then have plenty on hand. Plan for 2 drinks per hour per person during the first 2 hours and one drink per hour per person for every hour thereafter. Plan for each guest to trade a dirty glass for a clean one at least once. This is not a rule but a general guideline. Don't worry if you have a limited number of glasses in your cupboard; renting is always an option. Allow $1/2$ pound of ice per person (assuming the beverages are already chilled) for the first 2 hours and 1 pound for a party that will last 3 or more hours. Allow one pound of ice per person if the beverages need to be iced. Additional ice is needed if the party is outdoors and the weather is warm.

To stock up on liquor, start with calculating the total number of drinks you will be serving and then consider the following:

A 750-milliliter bottle (standard-size bottle of wine, champagne, or liquor) will yield six 4-ounce glasses. The same size bottle of spirits or liqueur will yield approximately sixteen $1^{1}/_{2}$-ounce shots of liquor for a mixed or straight drink. A 12-ounce portion of beer essentially serves one.

Unfortunately, if you have a full bar, there is no way to determine what guests will drink, so knowing how much of each type of liquor you'll need becomes a guesstimate. If possible, purchase at least one 750-milliliter bottle each of vodka, rum, scotch, bourbon, tequila, and gin. Purchase nonalcoholic beer and mixers such as fruit juices, tonic water, club soda, flavored sodas, and lime juice in small bottles so that unopened bottles can be stored until the next party. Purchase enough wine, champagne, and beer so that every guest could potentially drink one or two glasses of each.

Make an assessment of the crowd you will be entertaining. Ask yourself whether they are rowdy or conservative. The type of crowd will indicate how much liquor will be consumed. Also consider the day of the week and length of the party. People tend to drink more as the weekend nears.

When in doubt about how much food or drink you will need, err on the side of abundance. You can always eat leftovers, and most alcohol has a friendly shelf life. (Liquor will last a very long time even after it is opened. White wine that is uncorked can be refrigerated and consumed within 1 week. Red wine that is uncorked should be consumed within a day or two and remember that it can be used, for the frugal cook, as a cooking wine for up to a week. Beer should be consumed within a couple of months.)

Last but not least, finger food doesn't require utensils, but napkins are a necessity. Allow about 4 paper cocktail napkins per person per hour for food and drinks, and 1 to 2 linen napkins if you want to use cloth. Plates aren't necessary if you are passing food or serving it at strategic locations throughout the party. If you are planning a buffet table or only one location for food, plates allow people to get something to eat and still mingle. Use small paper or china plates that are 4 to 6 inches in size; anything larger is awkward and makes balancing plate and glass a difficult task for your guests.

first impressions

Presenting your food attractively is easy. Just use a little imagination and don't be afraid to improvise. If you don't have traditional serving platters, you can utilize small plates, unusual trays, decorative ceramic pieces, baskets, clear glass pieces, mirrors, wooden cutting boards, marble platters, and flat, wide bowls. You can disguise less-than-attractive pieces with paper doilies, linen napkins, large leaves (be certain that they are food friendly, not poisonous), edible flowers, or scattered fresh herbs.

For small, intimate groups that will be seated for most of the party, set food within arms' reach. Place food on several tables around the sides and center of the group. For large groups in a contained space, use a buffet arrangement for most dishes and then pass the remaining items. For a party that will be spread out in a large space, place dishes grouped together in several places so that guests can nosh as they mingle.

pairing principles

This book is divided into three chapters that marry food and drinks based on flavor intensity. In the first chapter, "Big and Bold," the recipes are meant to be paired with cocktails brimming with alcohol, from a Manhattan to a glass of Cabernet Sauvignon. In "Not Too Strong, Not Too Weak," the recipes will complement a mixed bar, from a cocktail that is more mixer than liquor to a full-bodied ale. The last chapter, "Light and Delicate," showcases recipes for finger foods that will match the subtle nuances of champagne, sparkling wine, a light-flavored spirit, or an effervescent lager.

Use these suggestions for planning your party or for pairing food with drinks based on what you like. If you want to create specific matches between plate and glass, keep in mind the following criteria:

Consider the alcohol content of the drink. Libations that pack a wallop of alcohol need to be tamed with food that is big in taste. Pick foods that are strong flavored or hearty in substance. For example, a pungent cheese will pair well with a robust red wine but will overwhelm a glass of Dubonnet and soda; spiced lamb will complement a Rob Roy but will overpower a white wine spritzer.

Balance texture and flavor. Consider how both the drink and the selected food will feel in your mouth. Will they come crashing in and take your taste buds hostage, or will they sneak in and glide out with a quiet announcement of their presence? Select matches that neither overpower nor mask each other, such as lemon-accented asparagus with sparkling wine.

Remember that opposites attract. Pair food and drinks that will comple-ment each other. Cut the richness of an hors d'oeuvre with a crisp bever-age; tame the spice of a fiery bite with a sweet elixir; or balance a salty food with a fruity potion. For example, seasoned meat or seafood with a spicy sauce will taste great with a slightly sweet blended margarita or fruit beer.

party-planning guidelines

The following chart is an at-a-glance guide for cocktail-party essentials. These are guideline but not rules. As a host, you will find that every party varies. At one party you might entertain ten people who eat and drink with gusto. At another party you may be entertaining eighteen people who eat and drink as though they were all on a diet. Use this chart as a starting point for determining how much of any one item you will need to purchase.

note: This chart is calculated on the assumption that heavy hors d'oeuvres are dinner. In other words, the host is filling up the guests because there are no plans for a more substantial dinner later.

yields: One 750-milliliter bottle of wine or champagne = Six 4-ounce servings
One 12-ounce container of beer = one serving
One 750-milliliter bottle liquor = Sixteen $1^1/_2$-ounce servings

	PARTY LENGTH		
4 GUESTS	I HOUR	I ½ HOURS	2 HOURS
(PRE-DINNER COCKTAILS)			
ITEM: ONE TYPE OF			
ALCOHOL SERVED			
wine/champagne (750-milliliter bottles):	2	2	3
or beer (12-ounce containers):	8	10	12
or one type liquor (750-milliliter bottles):	1	2	2
glasses:	6	6	8
napkins:	16	20	24
hors d'oeuvres (pieces):	16	24	32

	PARTY LENGTH		
12 GUESTS	I HOUR	2 ½ HOURS	3 HOURS
(HORS D'OEUVRES)			
ITEM: FULL BAR			
wine/champagne (750-milliliter bottles):	4	6	8
and beer (12-ounce containers):	24	32	36
and one type liquor (750-milliliter bottles):	2	2	3
glasses:	18	24	36
napkins:	36	48	60
hors d'oeuvres (pieces):	120	138	156

big and bold

big-flavored finger foods to match high-octane, high-alcohol cocktails

POWERFUL CHEESES, ROBUST PEPPERS, MUSCULAR NUTS, STRONG AROMATICS, earthy mushrooms, and fiery sauces: this chapter is bursting with flavors that pack a wallop. They go into the ring swinging, just itching to spar with a cocktail of equal strength. Don't be shy with the jigger or the corkscrew. Open your heartiest red wines, mix your meanest martini, and pour your sexiest highball. These foods deserve a party.

Need an idea? Try a Martini Soiree or a Highball Spree:

a martini soiree

The image alone is enough to make your mouth water: that frosted glass filled with shimmering liquid; that first icy sip of gin; and that reward of a tasty olive when you drain the last sip. So stop thinking about it and start gathering a few pals to indulge in the swankest of cocktails.

Invite six friends over for a couple of hours to indulge in some martinis and morsels. Rent or borrow the glasses (or splurge and invest in a fun set of martini glasses—you won't regret it). Purchase one bottle each of gin, vodka, and vermouth. Throw in a flavored vodka if you are feeling adventurous. Provide plenty of ice; three pounds should do. And stock up on the fun accoutrements: plain and gourmet stuffed olives, pickled onions, lemon and orange twists.

And for the perfect menu, plan on preparing a half batch of the following hor d'oeuvres: Nutty Napoleons (page 29), which can be assembled in advance and left at room temperature; Trout Tassies (page 47), crisp, cool, yet smoky hors d'oeuvres; Li'l Dumplins (page 40), spicy, intensely flavorful hot morsels that are always crowd pleasers.

a highball spree

The tinkle of ice, the sizzle of soda, the splash of your favorite liquor, this is the essence of a highball. It rests comfortably in your palm like the handshake of a good friend. There is no better excuse for inviting a group of ten over on a weekend evening than mixing up a batch of drinks, whether they are time-proven concoctions or your own inventions.

For a three-hour party, stock at least 25 glasses, 5 pounds of ice, and 50 cocktail napkins. Provide at least one bottle each of bourbon, scotch, gin, tequila, vodka, and rum. Fill in the bar with an assortment of mixers, from orange and lime juice to tonic water and flavored sodas. If you are feeling decadent, add olives, pickled onions, celery sticks, lemons, limes, and orange slices. Oh, and don't forget the swizzle sticks!

Complement your bar with a menu of Wonton Wonders (page 50), a fiery chicken salad inside a wonton cup that can be made in advance and served at room temperature. Add Lamb on a Limb (page 34), which will provide a hearty respite, and a double batch of Teardrops (page 45), which can be prepared ahead of time and reheated before serving. In that case, make two batches of each recipe. Remember, offer something hearty in addition to these finger foods to complete the meal—perhaps a crudités and cheese platter.

bayou biscuits

ANDOUILLE SAUSAGE BISCUITS

These Cajun-inspired biscuits are even better than the Smithfield ham biscuits that we grew up loving. We always use cake flour in our biscuits, just like Mom, because the results are lighter and flakier.

1½ cups cake flour

2 teaspoons garlic powder

2 teaspoons dried oregano

2 teaspoons dried thyme

2 teaspoons sugar

1¾ teaspoons baking powder

1½ teaspoons paprika

¼ teaspoon kosher salt

3 tablespoons cold unsalted butter
  cut into pea-size pieces

¾ cup heavy cream

4 ounces andouille sausage, cut
  into ¼-inch slices

¼ cup mayonnaise

Preheat the oven to 400°F.

Combine the flour, garlic powder, oregano, thyme, sugar, baking powder, paprika, and kosher salt in a food processor using the pulse setting. Add the butter and pulse a few times. Add the cream and process just until a ball is formed, no longer. Turn out the dough onto a floured board and knead briefly. Roll the dough out about ¼-inch thick. Cut into 1½-inch circles using a floured cookie cutter. Place on a parchment paper–lined baking sheet. Bake until lightly browned, 10 to 15 minutes.

Heat a large skillet over medium heat. Add the sausage and cook until brown and crisp around the edges. Transfer to a paper towel–lined plate to cool.

to assemble: Preheat the oven to 350°F. Cut the biscuits in half. Place the mayonnaise in a sealable plastic bag and squeeze the mayonnaise into one corner. Cut a small tip off the corner and pipe even amounts of mayonnaise onto both sides of each biscuit. Place a sausage slice on the bottom half of each biscuit. Cover with the top half. Place the sandwiches on a baking sheet and bake until warm, 5 to 7 minutes.

do-ahead tips: The biscuits can be frozen (unbaked) up to 1 week in advance. Thaw before baking. The biscuits can be baked up to 1 day in advance and stored at room temperature. They can be assembled and left at room temperature for up to 3 hours or frozen up to 1 week in advance and thawed before warming as directed.

yield: ABOUT 48 BISCUITS

delhi blues

BLUE CHEESE AND WALNUT SHORTBREAD WITH CHUTNEY

This savory version of shortbread offers a sensational combination of rich blue cheese and tangy chutney, an Indian condiment typically made with mangoes. If your time is limited, you can serve the shortbread crackers without the toppings. They will still be a crowd pleaser.

$1/2$ cup sharp blue cheese (such as Maytag), at room temperature

3 tablespoons unsalted butter, at room temperature

$1/2$ cup all-purpose flour

$1/4$ cup cornstarch

$1/4$ teaspoon pepper

$1/4$ teaspoon kosher salt

$1/3$ cup walnuts, chopped

3 tablespoons cream cheese

3 tablespoons chutney, preferably Major Grey's (see Note)

$1/2$ cup walnut halves, toasted for garnishing

36 parsley leaves for garnishing

Combine the blue cheese and butter in a food processor; process until creamy. Mix the flour, cornstarch, pepper, and kosher salt together in a small bowl; add to the blue cheese mixture. Pulse to combine. Add the chopped walnuts and process just until incorporated. Do not overprocess. Remove the blue cheese mixture from the food processor bowl and shape into a ball; cover with plastic wrap. Refrigerate until firm, at least one hour.

Preheat the oven to 325°F.

Place the chilled dough on a piece of plastic wrap and cover with another piece of plastic wrap. Roll the dough out about $1/8$-inch thick. Remove the plastic wrap and cut into 1-inch circles using a fluted cookie cutter. Place on a parchment paper–lined baking sheet. Repeat until all the dough is used. Bake until light brown, about 25 minutes. Let cool.

(continued)

to assemble: Spread $1/4$ teaspoon of the cream cheese on each short-bread. Top with equal amounts of chutney, a walnut half, and a leaf of parsley.

do-ahead tips: The shortbread can be prepared up to 3 days in advance and stored in an airtight container. Assemble up to 1 hour before serving.

note: We like to use Sharwood's Major Grey's chutney because of its unique tangy taste. It is available in most supermarkets and grocery stores.

yield: ABOUT 36 SHORTBREAD CRACKERS

mary's little lambs

FILO CUPS WITH SPICED LAMB, MINT, AND FETA

Don't be intimidated working with filo—these pastry cups are really quite simple. While working, cover the unused filo with plastic wrap and a damp dish towel to prevent it from drying out.

6 sheets filo dough, each trimmed to 12 by 16 inches and cut into 48 two-inch squares (stack the sheets and cut them all at once)

2 tablespoons butter, melted

1 tablespoon vegetable oil

1 cup chopped onions

2 tablespoons minced garlic

$^1/_2$ teaspoon kosher salt

$^1/_4$ teaspoon pepper

8 ounces lean ground lamb

$^1/_2$ cup black currants

$1^1/_4$ teaspoons ground cumin

$^3/_4$ teaspoon ground ginger

$^3/_4$ teaspoon cinnamon

$^1/_4$ teaspoon allspice

$^1/_4$ cup julienned fresh mint

$^1/_4$ cup crumbled feta

Preheat the oven to 350°F.

Mold 3 filo squares into the bottom of a miniature (1-inch) muffin tin. Place 3 more filo squares at a 45-degree angle on top and press gently into the muffin cups. Brush lightly with melted butter. Cook until lightly golden brown, 4 to 6 minutes. Let cool. Place on a baking sheet and cover tightly with plastic wrap until ready to use.

Heat the oil in a medium nonstick skillet over medium heat. Add the onions and garlic. Season with $^1/_4$ teaspoon of the kosher salt and $^1/_8$ teaspoon of the pepper. Cook until the onions are tender, 5 to 7 minutes. Add the lamb, black currants, cumin, ginger, cinnamon, allspice, remaining $^1/_4$ teaspoon kosher salt, and remaining $^1/_8$ teaspoon pepper. Cook until the lamb is cooked through, about 5 minutes. Stir in the mint.

to assemble: Place 1 heaping teaspoon of the lamb mixture in each filo cup. Top with a heaping $^1/_4$ teaspoon feta. Serve while the filling is warm.

(continued)

big and bold

do-ahead tips: The filo cups can be prepared up to 5 days in advance and stored in an airtight container. The filling can be prepared up to 2 days in advance and refrigerated. (Do not add the mint until assembly.) The cups can be filled up to 1 hour in advance and warmed in a 300°F oven for 5 minutes.

yield: 48 FILLED FILO CUPS

oink!

The contrast between hot and cold makes this Caribbean-influenced dish a winner. The chilled yet slightly fiery mango dipping sauce is a refreshing dip for the jerk-flavored pork. For an innovative presentation, cut the top off of a red bell pepper and use it as a bowl for the mango dipping sauce (cut a thin slice off the bottom of the pepper so that it will lie flat; use a spoon to scrape out the seeds and ribs).

DIPPING SAUCE:

1 cup coarsely chopped mango

2 tablespoons pineapple juice

2 teaspoons lime juice

$1^1/_4$ teaspoons kosher salt

2 tablespoons chopped red onion

1 tablespoon chopped fresh cilantro

1 teaspoon chopped green jalapeño, seeds included

1 pound boneless pork loin, trimmed and cut into $^3/_4$-inch cubes

1 large red bell pepper, cut into $^3/_4$-inch squares

2 tablespoons olive oil

2 teaspoons paprika

2 teaspoons onion powder

2 teaspoons cinnamon

1 teaspoon allspice

36 five-inch bamboo skewers (see Note)

Preheat the oven to 450°F.

to make the dipping sauce: Place the mango, pineapple juice, lime juice, and $^1/_4$ teaspoon of the kosher salt in a blender and process until well blended but not smooth. Pour into a bowl and add the onion, cilantro, and jalapeño. Mix well. Refrigerate until chilled.

Place the pork and bell pepper in a medium bowl; drizzle with the olive oil. Mix the paprika, onion powder, cinnamon, allspice, and the remaining 1 teaspoon kosher salt together in a small bowl; add to the pork. Toss to coat until the spices are evenly distributed.

(continued)

big and bold

to assemble: Slide a piece of red pepper, skin-side first, onto a skewer, followed by a piece of pork. Repeat until all of the ingredients have been used. Place on a foil-lined baking sheet and bake until meat is barely cooked in the center, 10 to 15 minutes. Serve with the mango dipping sauce.

do-ahead tips: The dipping sauce can be prepared up to 1 day in advance (it will thicken; add pineapple juice until it reaches a desired consistency). Assemble the skewers up to 1 day in advance (omit the salt from the spice mixture and season with salt just prior to cooking). Bake as directed.

note: Soak the bamboo skewers in water for at least fifteen minutes before using to prevent splintering and burning.

yield: ABOUT 36 SKEWERS

big and bold

smoked salmon bonbons

SMOKED SALMON AND CREAM CHEESE CROQUETTES

Bonbon is the French word for candy, which is appropriate because these creamy, rich croquettes redefine the phrase "melt in your mouth." Serve them with a citrus vodka martini or with a gin fizz at brunch. One bit of advice: Always make far more than you think you will need. These go fast.

12 ounces cream cheese,
  at room temperature

6 ounces thinly sliced smoked
  salmon, coarsely chopped

1/4 cup chopped green onions

2 tablespoons chopped fresh dill

1 tablespoon plus 1 teaspoon
  horseradish

2 teaspoons lemon juice

1/4 teaspoon freshly ground
  pepper

1/2 cup all-purpose flour

1 egg, beaten

2 cups fresh bread crumbs

Peanut oil for frying

Combine the cream cheese, salmon, green onions, dill, horseradish, lemon juice, and pepper in a food processor. Process just until blended. Drop the salmon mixture by scant tablespoons onto a parchment paper–lined baking sheet. Cover with plastic wrap and refrigerate until firm, about 30 minutes.

Put the flour, egg, and bread crumbs in three separate bowls. Dredge the salmon balls in the flour to coat completely. Shake off any excess flour. Shape into neat spheres. Dip into the egg and then the bread crumbs. Place the finished croquettes on a baking sheet. When all of the croquettes are finished, cover with plastic wrap and refrigerate until chilled, at least 20 minutes.

Fill a large saucepan 2 1/2 inches deep with the peanut oil. Heat the oil to 350°F. Add the croquettes in batches and cook until crispy and golden brown, about 2 minutes. Transfer the croquettes to a paper towel–lined baking sheet to absorb excess oil. Serve hot.

do-ahead tips: The salmon mixture can be prepared up to 1 day in advance and refrigerated. The croquettes can be coated up to 3 hours in advance and refrigerated or frozen up to 2 weeks in advance (if frozen, let thaw 45 minutes before frying). The croquettes can be fried up to 3 hours in advance and warmed in a 350°F oven for 5 to 7 minutes.

yield: ABOUT 36 CROQUETTES

nutty napoleons

TOASTED PECAN AND ENGLISH STILTON NAPOLEONS

These bite-sized sandwiches are ambrosia for cheese and nut lovers. And the presentation is impressive for such a simple-to-prepare hors d'oeuvre. If you reduce the recipe, do not use a food processor; make the cheese mixture by hand. Chop extra chives and sprinkle them onto a plate as a colorful backdrop for the napoleons.

96 (about 5 ounces) perfect pecan halves

3 ounces cream cheese, at room temperature

2 ounces Stilton cheese, at room temperature

2 teaspoons port

$^1/_2$ teaspoon honey

Pinch of cracked black pepper

2 tablespoons chopped fresh chives, for garnishing

big and bold

Preheat the oven to 350°F.

Place the pecans on a baking sheet. Bake until brown and aromatic, 7 to 10 minutes. Remove from the oven and let cool.

Combine the cream cheese, Stilton, port, honey, and pepper in a food processor. Process until smooth. Transfer to a sealable plastic bag and squeeze mixture into one corner.

to assemble: Spread 24 pecan halves flat-side down on the sheet tray. Cut a small tip off the corner of the bag of cheese mixture. Pipe about $^1/_4$ teaspoon of the cheese mixture evenly onto each pecan half. Top with a second pecan, flat-side down, and pipe about $^1/_4$ teaspoon of the cheese mixture onto each napoleon. Sprinkle with chopped chives to garnish.

do-ahead tips: The pecans can be toasted up to 3 days in advance and stored in an airtight container. The Stilton mixture can be prepared up to 3 days in advance and refrigerated; bring it to room temperature before assembly. Assemble up to 3 hours in advance and let sit at room temperature.

yield: 48 NAPOLEONS

chèvre champignons

MUSHROOMS STUFFED WITH GOAT CHEESE, SPINACH, AND BACON

This is a foolproof recipe for pleasing a crowd. Time and time again, guests at our parties come rushing back to the kitchen in pursuit of the recipe for these rich and decadent hors d'oeuvres. Select mushrooms that are slightly larger than bite-size because they will shrink a little when they are cooked, but anything bigger can become messy.

4 tablespoons plus 2 teaspoons bacon grease or olive oil

1 cup chopped onion

$3/4$ teaspoon kosher salt

$1/2$ teaspoon pepper

8 ounces goat cheese, at room temperature

2 tablespoons heavy cream

$1/4$ teaspoon ground nutmeg

One 10-ounce package frozen chopped spinach, thawed

$1/2$ pound bacon, cooked and finely chopped

36 white mushrooms, uniform in size, stems removed

Preheat the oven to 350°F.

Heat 2 teaspoons of the bacon grease in a medium nonstick skillet over medium heat. Add the onion and season with $1/4$ teaspoon of the kosher salt and $1/8$ teaspoon of the pepper. Cook until the onion is tender, 5 to 7 minutes. Transfer to a medium bowl and let cool. When cool, add the goat cheese, cream, and nutmeg, and $1/8$ teaspoon of the pepper. Stir until well mixed.

Squeeze the spinach with your hands to remove any excess liquid. Add spinach and bacon to the onion mixture. Refrigerate until ready to use.

Heat 2 more tablespoons of the bacon grease in a large nonstick skillet over medium heat. Add half of the mushrooms and season with $1/4$ teaspoon of the kosher salt and $1/8$ teaspoon of the pepper. Cook the mushrooms until golden brown and tender, about 4 minutes per side. Transfer to a paper towel–lined baking sheet, top-side up. Wipe the skillet using a paper towel and return to the heat. Add the remaining 2 tablespoons bacon grease and heat. Add the remaining mushrooms and season with the remaining $1/4$ teaspoon kosher salt and the remaining $1/8$ teaspoon pepper. Transfer to the baking sheet with the other mushrooms.

to assemble: Place 1 heaping teaspoon of the spinach filling in the center of the bottom of each mushroom. Bake until warm, 5 to 7 minutes; serve warm.

do-ahead tips: The spinach filling can be prepared up to 2 days in advance and refrigerated. The mushrooms can also be assembled up to 2 days in advance and refrigerated. Bake as directed.

yield: 36 STUFFED MUSHROOMS

big and bold

WISDOM

open sesame shrimp

Showcase these shrimp with kamikazes. When serving this dish, be sure to set out a small container for the tails and place a tail in it so guests follow the example.

DIPPING SAUCE:

1/2 cup mayonnaise

1/3 cup tahini

2 tablespoons mirin (sweet rice wine)

2 tablespoons soy sauce

2 tablespoons seasoned rice vinegar

2 tablespoons lime juice

2 tablespoons grated peeled fresh ginger

1 tablespoon sesame oil

24 medium (about 1 pound) shrimp, peeled and deveined, tails intact

2 teaspoons vegetable oil

1/4 teaspoon kosher salt

1/8 teaspoon freshly ground pepper

1 tablespoon black sesame seeds or 2 tablespoons white sesame seeds

big and bold

to make the dipping sauce: Combine the mayonnaise, tahini, mirin, soy sauce, rice vinegar, lime juice, grated ginger, and sesame oil in a food processor and process until smooth. Refrigerate until chilled, about 2 hours.

Preheat the oven to 450°F.

Toss the shrimp in a bowl with the oil, kosher salt, and pepper. Dip one side of each shrimp in the sesame seeds. Place on a foil-lined baking sheet, sesame seed–side up. Bake until the shrimp are opaque, 5 to 7 minutes. Serve warm with the dipping sauce.

do-ahead tips: The dipping sauce can be prepared 3 days in advance. The shrimp can be prepared up to 8 hours in advance and refrigerated.

yield: 24 SHRIMP

lamb on a limb

LAMB SKEWERS WITH MINT-MUSTARD DIPPING SAUCE

The mint and mustard combination really enhances the rich lamb. Make a border of rosemary sprigs around the serving dish. Don't forget to place a small glass out for dispensing the toothpicks.

1/4 cup vegetable oil

1/4 cup finely chopped onion

2 tablespoons red wine

2 tablespoons fresh rosemary leaves

2 garlic cloves

1 tablespoon Dijon mustard

3/4 pound boneless trimmed lamb loin, cut in half lengthwise if more than 2 3/4 inches wide

DIPPING SAUCE:

1/4 cup Dijon mustard

1/4 cup crème fraîche

2 tablespoons mint jelly

pinch of kosher salt

1/8 teaspoon pepper

1/4 teaspoon kosher salt

1/8 teaspoon pepper

1 tablespoon vegetable oil

24 wooden toothpicks

Combine 1/4 cup oil, onion, red wine, rosemary, garlic, and 1 tablespoon mustard in a blender. Blend until smooth. Place the lamb in a sealable plastic bag; add the marinade and seal. Refrigerate at least 2 hours and not longer than 24 hours.

to make the dipping sauce: Combine 1/4 cup mustard, the crème fraîche, mint jelly, pinch of kosher salt, and 1/8 teaspoon pepper in a small bowl. Whisk to combine. Set aside.

Season the lamb with the remaining 1/4 teaspoon kosher salt and 1/8 teaspoon pepper. Heat the remaining 1 tablespoon vegetable oil in a large skillet over high heat. Add the lamb and sear until evenly browned, about 3 minutes on each side. Transfer the lamb to a cutting board, cover with foil, and let rest for 10 minutes.

to assemble: Cut the lamb into thin slices, about $1/8$ inch thick. Fold each slice to create a ribbon effect and slide onto a toothpick. Repeat until all of the slices have been skewered. Serve immediately with the dipping sauce.

do-ahead tips: The lamb can be cooked and refrigerated, unsliced, up to 1 day in advance. Assemble up to 1 hour in advance, cover tightly with foil, and warm in a 350°F oven for 3 to 5 minutes.

yield: ABOUT 24 SKEWERED LAMB SLICES

big and bold

puff the magic mushroom

PUFF PASTRY WITH CREMINI MUSHROOM FILLING

Puff pastry should be a staple in everyone's freezer because it is a user-friendly companion ingredient for both sweet and savory recipes. In this recipe, its buttery taste and ethereal texture are the perfect complements to the earthy mushroom filling. One bite and you'll feel like frolicking in the land of Honnalee.

One 10-by-10-inch sheet puff pastry, thawed and rolled out $1/8$ inch thick

1 egg, lightly beaten

4 tablespoons ($1/2$ stick) unsalted butter

4 cups sliced cremini mushrooms

$1/2$ teaspoon kosher salt

$1/4$ teaspoon pepper

$3/4$ cup chopped onion

$1/4$ cup dry white wine

$1/4$ cup crème fraîche

2 tablespoons grated Parmesan cheese

2 teaspoons chopped fresh thyme

Preheat the oven to 400°F.

Lay the puff pastry on a lightly floured surface. Trim the sides to form an 8-inch square. Cut into 36 squares. Place on a parchment paper–lined baking sheet and brush with the egg. Bake until golden, 10 to 12 minutes. Let cool. Reduce the oven temperature to 350°F.

Heat 3 tablespoons of the butter in a large nonstick skillet over medium heat. Add the mushrooms and season with $1/4$ teaspoon of the kosher salt and $1/8$ teaspoon of the pepper. Cook until the mushrooms begin to turn brown and crispy, 7 to 10 minutes. Transfer to a small bowl.

Wipe out the skillet and return to the stove. Heat the remaining 1 tablespoon butter over medium heat. Add the onions and season with the remaining $1/4$ teaspoon kosher salt and the remaining $1/8$ teaspoon pepper.

Cook until tender, about 5 minutes. Add the wine and cook until the liquid is absorbed, 3 to 5 minutes.

Put the mushrooms, onions, crème fraîche, Parmesan, and thyme in a food processor. Pulse 3 or 4 times until mixture is combined but not pureed.

to assemble: Cut each puff pastry square in half crosswise. Place about $^1/_2$ teaspoon of the mushroom mixture on one half of each square and top with the remaining pastry half. Bake until warm, about 5 minutes. Serve warm.

do-ahead tips: The puff pastry can be baked up to 2 days in advance, covered tightly with plastic wrap, and stored at room temperature. The mushroom filling can be prepared up to 2 days in advance and refrigerated. The hors d'oeuvres can be assembled up to 3 hours in advance. Bake as directed.

yield: 36 FILLED PASTRIES

sorry, charlie

SPICY TUNA TARTARE ON WONTON SQUARES

Even the staunchest of sushi opponents are won over by this robust flavor combination. Purchase only sashimi-quality tuna when preparing this recipe. Look for it at upscale supermarkets and specialty seafood stores.

1 tablespoon vegetable oil

Twelve 3-by-3^1/$_2$-inch square wonton wrappers, cut into quarters

10 ounces sashimi-quality tuna, cut into ^{1}/$_8$-inch dice, chilled

3 tablespoons chopped green onions, green part only

3 tablespoons pine nuts, toasted

1 tablespoon plus 1 teaspoon soy sauce

1 tablespoon sesame oil

1^1/$_2$ teaspoons chopped jalapeño, seeds removed

1 teaspoon grated peeled fresh ginger

Preheat the oven to 350°F.

Brush a baking sheet with the oil. Arrange the wonton squares on the baking sheet. Bake until golden brown, 8 to 10 minutes. Let cool.

Mix the tuna, green onions, pine nuts, soy sauce, sesame oil, jalapeño, and ginger together in a medium bowl. Mix well. Use immediately. Do not mix in advance.

to assemble: Place 1 heaping teaspoon of the tuna mixture on each wonton square. Serve immediately. It is very important that the tuna is very cold.

do-ahead tips: The wonton squares can be baked up to 3 days in advance and stored in an airtight container. The tuna can be diced up to 12 hours in advance and refrigerated.

yield: 48 TOPPED WONTONS

big and bold

li'l dumplins

EGGPLANT AND SAUSAGE DUMPLINGS WITH SESAME-PLUM SAUCE

Roasting the eggplant over a hot flame creates an unforgettable fire-roasted filling for these dumplings—try them and you will be hooked on this method time and time again.

DIPPING SAUCE:

One 8-ounce jar plum sauce (see Note)

1 teaspoon lime juice

$^1/_2$ teaspoon sesame oil

1 small to medium (about 1 pound) eggplant

2 teaspoons olive oil

$^3/_4$ cup finely chopped onion

$^1/_4$ teaspoon kosher salt

Pinch of pepper

$^1/_2$ pound ground pork sausage

$^3/_4$ teaspoon ground cumin

$^1/_2$ teaspoon ground coriander

$^1/_4$ teaspoon ground ginger

50 square wonton wrappers, trimmed into 2$^1/_2$-inch squares

1 egg white, lightly beaten

Vegetable oil for frying

to make the sauce: Combine the plum sauce, lime juice, and sesame oil. Refrigerate.

Prick the eggplant 5 times with a toothpick and remove any leaves from around the stem. Place directly on a high gas flame. Cook, rotating, until the flesh is soft and the skin is black and crisp, about 12 minutes. Transfer to a shallow bowl. Let cool.

Heat the olive oil in a medium nonstick skillet over medium heat. Add the onions and season with $^1/_8$ teaspoon of the kosher salt and pepper. Cook until the onions are tender, about 5 minutes. Transfer to a medium bowl.

Return the skillet to the stove and heat over high heat. Add the sausage and cook until completely brown, about 6 minutes. Transfer the sausage to a paper towel–lined plate using a slotted spoon.

Peel the eggplant and discard the liquid and any hard seeds. Gently squeeze the flesh to remove any excess liquid and chop coarsely. Place 1 cup eggplant, onions, sausage, cumin, coriander, ginger, and remaining $^1/_8$ teaspoon kosher salt in a food processor. Pulse a few times until well mixed. Refrigerate until ready to assemble.

Lay the wontons, 3 at a time, on a work surface. Brush the edges with the egg white. Place 1 teaspoon of the eggplant mixture onto the center of each wonton. Pull the opposing corners together and pinch lightly. Pull the remaining sides up and press all four corners together. Be sure to seal the edges to prevent the filling from escaping. Repeat until all of the ingredients have been used. Place on a parchment paper–lined baking sheet.

Fill a large saucepan $2^1/_2$ inches deep with vegetable oil. Heat to 350°F. Add the dumplings in small batches and cook until crispy, about 2 minutes. Transfer to a paper towel–lined baking sheet. Serve hot with the sesame-plum sauce.

do-ahead tips: The plum sauce can be prepared up to 3 days in advance. The eggplant filling can be prepared up to 2 days in advance. The dumplings can be assembled and frozen up to 2 weeks in advance and fried frozen. The dumplings can be fried up to 3 hours in advance and warmed in a 400°F oven until crisp.

note: We have discovered that store-bought plum sauces vary dramatically in flavor, ranging from very sweet and pungent to bland. Always taste the plum sauce before using it in a recipe. Adjust the lime juice and sesame oil in this recipe if necessary to create a balance of sweet, sour, and spice. If the plum sauce you purchase is too sweet, add peeled, minced fresh ginger or soy sauce for a balanced flavor.

yield: 50 DUMPLINGS

eggstravaganza!

DEVILED EGGS WITH CAVIAR

This updated deviled egg takes out the evil, leaving you with only the D, as in delicious. The saltiness of the caviar and the rich, creamy filling are the perfect antidote for a strong drink—or serve as an elegant start to a brunch with a mimosa.

6 small eggs, cold	$^1/_2$ teaspoon minced lemon zest
2$^1/_4$ teaspoons kosher salt	1 tablespoon high-quality caviar
$^1/_4$ cup sour cream	Twenty-four $^3/_4$-inch-long chive tips
3 tablespoons minced onion	
2 teaspoons lemon juice	

Place the eggs in a medium saucepan. Add enough water to cover the eggs by more than $1^1/_2$ inches. Add 2 teaspoons of the kosher salt (salt makes peeling the eggs easier). Bring to a boil over high heat. Remove from the heat, cover, and let sit for 12 minutes. Pour out the hot water. Rinse the eggs under cold running water for 2 to 3 minutes. Pour out any excess water and shake the pan to roll the eggs so that they collide and the shells crack. Cover with cold water. Peel under running water, rinsing off any remaining pieces of shell. Cut a thin slice off the top and bottom of each egg; be careful not to cut into the yolk. Cut the eggs in half cross-wise, not lengthwise. Remove the yolks and place in a small bowl. Arrange the whites, flat-side down, on a serving platter.

Combine the yolks with the sour cream, onion, lemon juice, lemon zest, and the remaining $^1/_4$ teaspoon kosher salt in a small bowl using a fork. Mash until creamy and well blended.

to assemble: Place the yolk mixture in a sealable plastic bag and squeeze into one corner. Cut a $^1/_4$-inch tip off the corner and pipe even amounts into the egg whites until filled. Top each egg with $^1/_4$ teaspoon caviar. Garnish with 2 chive tips set in a crisscross design. Serve immediately.

do-ahead tips: The eggs can be cooked and filled up to 1 day in advance and refrigerated. Return to room temperature for about 2 hours. When ready to serve, garnish with the caviar and chives.

yield: 12 EGG HALVES

popeye poppers

SPINACH AND SMOKED GOUDA SPHERES

These bold and decadent morsels bursting with flavor make it a pleasure to eat Popeye's favorite food. Check your market's deli section or specialty food stores for high-quality cheeses, and ask for a sample before making your purchase. You must use top-quality smoked Gouda or this recipe will turn out wimpy.

2 teaspoons olive oil

1 cup chopped onion

1/4 teaspoon kosher salt

Pinch of pepper

One 10-ounce package frozen chopped spinach, thawed

1 1/4 cups dry bread crumbs

1/2 cup grated smoked Gouda

1/2 cup grated Parmesan

1 large egg

3 tablespoons salted butter, melted

1/8 teaspoon nutmeg

Preheat the oven to 350°F.

Heat the oil in a large nonstick skillet over medium heat. Add the onion and season with the kosher salt and pepper. Cook until tender, 5 to 7 minutes. Remove from heat.

Squeeze the spinach in your hands to remove all of the liquid. Put the spinach in a food processor. Add the onion, 1/2 cup of the bread crumbs, smoked Gouda, Parmesan, egg, butter, and nutmeg; process until completely combined and smooth.

Form 1-inch spheres with the spinach mixture and roll each sphere in the remaining 3/4 cup bread crumbs to coat completely. Place on a foil- or parchment paper–lined baking sheet. Bake until hot and lightly golden, about 10 minutes. Do not overcook or they will get dry.

do-ahead tips: The spinach spheres can be prepared and refrigerated up to 1 day in advance or frozen up to 1 week in advance. Let thaw before baking. Bake according to directions.

yield: ABOUT 36 SPINACH SPHERES

teardrops

We prefer to use challah bread for this recipe because of its texture, which creates an ethereal soufflé-like consistency when baked in this recipe. If you can't find challah, try using brioche or another egg-based bread.

$1/2$ cup (1 stick) unsalted butter

$1/3$ cup finely chopped onion

$1/8$ teaspoon kosher salt

$1/8$ teaspoon pepper

4 ounces cream cheese

$1/3$ cup firmly packed grated Jarlsberg cheese

3 tablespoons dehydrated minced onions

3 tablespoons chopped fresh chives

2 large egg whites

$3/4$ pound challah bread, crusts removed, cut into $3/4$-inch cubes

Preheat the oven to 350°F.

Heat 1 tablespoon of the butter in a small nonstick skillet over medium heat. Add the onion, kosher salt, and pepper and cook until tender, about 4 minutes.

Put the cream cheese, Jarlsberg, and dehydrated onions in the top of a double boiler set over hot water; cook until melted, stirring constantly. Remove from the heat and add the onions, the remaining 7 tablespoons butter, and the chives. Stir to mix well.

Beat the egg whites until stiff peaks form. Fold one quarter of the egg whites into the cheese mixture. Fold in the remaining egg whites. Dip the bread cubes, one at a time, into the cheese mixture and place on a foil- or parchment paper–lined baking sheet. Bake until the puffs are golden brown, about 15 minutes. Serve hot.

do-ahead tip: Freeze the puffs on a baking sheet and then transfer to a sealable plastic bag or container. Bake as directed, without thawing.

yield: ABOUT 24 ONION PUFFS

big and bold

trout tassies

SMOKED TROUT SALAD ON CUCUMBER SLICES

Tassies, or little cups, made from cucumbers make impressive carriers for savory fillings. For this recipe, if you can't find smoked trout, which is usually available in delicatessens and seafood stores, smoked salmon also works well. For an attractive presentation, run a zester lengthwise down the cucumber several times to create a striped effect before cutting the cucumber into slices.

1 cup (about 4^1/$_2$ ounces) chopped smoked trout

^{1}/$_3$ cup cream cheese, at room temperature

2 tablespoons heavy cream

2 tablespoons finely chopped red onion

2 teaspoons lemon juice

2 teaspoons finely chopped fresh dill

1 teaspoon chopped lemon zest

1^1/$_2$ teaspoons horseradish

^{1}/$_8$ teaspoon pepper

Kosher salt for seasoning

One 12-inch English cucumber, cut into forty-eight ^{1}/$_4$-inch slices, chilled

48 dill sprigs for garnishing

Mix the smoked trout, cream cheese, cream, onion, lemon juice, dill, lemon zest, horseradish, and pepper together in a small bowl. Season to taste with salt. Refrigerate until partially chilled.

to assemble: Place 1 teaspoon of the trout salad on each cucumber slice and garnish with a dill sprig.

do-ahead tips: The trout salad can be prepared up to 2 days in advance. The hors d'oeuvres can be assembled up to 1 hour in advance and refrigerated.

yield: 48 TOPPED CUCUMBER SLICES

steaked and thai-ed

SKEWERED THAI-STYLE STEAK WITH LIME, JALAPEÑO, AND MINT

This dish is inspired by a cold beef salad that we ate in Bangkok several years ago. It is known as yam nuea. *The sensation was so unforgettable that we have done our best to recreate the dish in skewer form. Don't forget to set out a container for used skewers.*

DIPPING SAUCE:

$^1/_3$ cup fresh lime juice

$^1/_4$ cup finely chopped red onion

2 teaspoons minced garlic

1 tablespoon sugar

1 tablespoon fish sauce (see Note)

1 tablespoon chopped jalapeño, with seeds

3 tablespoons vegetable oil

1 pound London broil, about 1 inch thick and 8 inches wide

Vegetable oil for brushing the meat

$^1/_2$ teaspoon kosher salt

$^1/_4$ teaspoon pepper

36 medium mint leaves for garnishing

36 five-inch bamboo skewers (see Note)

Preheat the grill to high heat.

to make the dipping sauce: Mix the lime juice, red onion, garlic, sugar, fish sauce, and jalapeño together in a small bowl. Add the oil slowly, while whisking. Refrigerate until chilled.

Brush both sides of the meat with vegetable oil and season with kosher salt and pepper. Grill until medium rare in the center, about 4 minutes per side. Remove from the grill and let rest for at least 15 minutes.

Cut the meat into uniform $^1/_8$-inch-thick slices, 3 to 4 inches long. Place a mint leaf on each slice and roll up. Slide onto a skewer. Serve with the dipping sauce.

do-ahead tips: The dipping sauce can be prepared up to 1 day in advance. The steak can be grilled and refrigerated unsliced up to 1 day in advance. The skewers can be assembled up to 8 hours in advance and refrigerated. Let sit at room temperature 30 minutes before serving.

note: Fish sauce, the ingredient that lends a distinctive flavor to this dish, is common in many Asian dishes. Look for fish sauce in the Asian sections of supermarkets or in specialty markets. If you can't find it, substitute 2 teaspoons Worcestershire sauce and 1 tablespoon soy sauce.

note: Soak the bamboo skewers in water for at least fifteen minutes before using to prevent splintering.

yield: ABOUT 36 SKEWERS

big and bold

wonton wonders

These one-biters are truly explosive with flavor due to a small amount of green curry paste. This store-bought blend of green chiles, garlic, onion, and spices is worth seeking out, as it is truly a potent secret ingredient.

12 wonton wrappers, cut into quarters

Vegetable oil for brushing the wontons

6 cups water

2 teaspoons kosher salt

1 pound (about 3 medium) boneless, skinless chicken breasts

1/4 cup Major Grey's chutney (see Note, page 20)

1/4 cup plus 2 tablespoons plain yogurt

3 tablespoons crunchy peanut butter

1 tablespoon fresh lime juice

1 1/2 teaspoons green curry paste (see Note)

1/4 cup chopped green onions for garnishing, green part only

Preheat the oven to 325°F.

Place the wontons on a work surface and brush lightly with the oil. Mold the wontons, oiled-side up, into the bottoms of miniature (1-inch) muffin tins. Bake until light brown, 5 to 7 minutes. Let cool slightly and remove from the muffin tins. Cool on a wire rack. Place on a baking sheet and cover tightly with plastic wrap until ready to assemble.

Heat the water and 1 1/2 teaspoons of the kosher salt in a medium saucepan over medium heat. Just before the water comes to a boil, add the chicken and simmer until cooked through, about 12 minutes. Transfer the chicken to a paper towel–lined plate and pat dry. Let cool slightly. Finely chop and season with the remaining 1/2 teaspoon kosher salt. Mix the chutney, yogurt, peanut butter, lime juice, and curry paste together in a medium bowl. Add the chicken and mix well. Refrigerate until slightly chilled.

to assemble: Place 1 heaping teaspoon of the chicken salad in each wonton cup and garnish with green onions.

do-ahead tips: The wonton cups can be baked up to 3 days in advance and stored in an airtight container. The chicken salad can be prepared up to 1 day in advance (let sit at room temperature for 30 minutes before serving). The wonton cups can be filled up to 1 hour in advance.

note: We like Thai Kitchen brand curry paste. Look for it in the Asian ingredient section of supermarkets, or call Epicurean International at 800-967-8424 for purchasing information. Or visit their Web site at www.thaikitchen.com.

yield: 48 WONTON CUPS

duck jubilee

GLAZED SMOKED DUCK WITH CHERRIES

This is a spectacular holiday hors d'oeuvre that will woo even the most sophisticated of guests. If you are short on oven space, serve this dish at room temperature with an arugula leaf rolled inside as a delicious alternative.

1 cup full-bodied red wine

1 cup red currant jam

$1/4$ teaspoon pepper

2 bay leaves

2 cinnamon sticks

48 (about $2/3$ cup) dried bing cherries

48 thin slices (about 10 ounces) smoked duck breast (see Note)

48 wooden toothpicks

Preheat oven to 350°F. Combine the red wine, jam, pepper, bay leaves, and cinnamon sticks together in a medium saucepan. Bring to a boil over medium heat. Reduce the heat, add the cherries, and let simmer until thickened into a glaze with the consistency of syrup, 15 to 20 minutes. Remove from the heat and drain, discarding the cinnamon sticks and the bay leaves. Set both the glaze and the plumped cherries aside.

Spread the duck slices on a work surface. Brush each duck slice lightly with the glaze and place 1 cherry on each slice. Roll each slice tightly and secure with a toothpick. Repeat until all of the slices are skewered. Place on a foil-lined baking sheet. Bake until warm, about 5 minutes. (As an alternative, place an arugula leaf on the duck before placing the cherries. Serve at room temperature.)

do-ahead tips: The glaze can be prepared up to 1 week in advance and refrigerated. Heat to return to a liquid consistency and strain out the cherries. The skewers can be assembled 2 days in advance. Warm as directed.

note: Our favorite smoked duck is produced by Grimaud Farms. Order it by calling Joie de Vivre at 800-648-8854. Another is D'Artagnan at 800-327-8246 or visit their Web site at www.dartagnan.com.

yield: 48 DUCK SKEWERS

not too strong, not too weak

well-balanced hors d'oeuvres that complement a range
of beverages, from daiquiris to gin and tonics

DYNAMIC SPICES, DAZZLING CAVIAR, CHARISMATIC CHEESES, ENERGETIC
herbs, and captivating peppers: these are the superstars of the hors
d'oeuvres world. They will entertain your party's palate and share the
spotlight with a full cast of cocktails. Why not host a premiere for these
tasty tidbits?

Entice your friends with a Beer Tasting, a Wine Revelry, or a Frozen Fête:

a beer tasting

A perfect pour from the bottle into the glass is just the start of a good
beer. From pilsners to pale ales, the flavors and "mouth feel" of all kinds
of beer pair well with a wide range of foods, from hot mustard to salty
tortilla chips. Take advantage of the marvelous selection of available

imported, domestic, and microbrewed beers by planning a party around them. Invite twelve people over and request that each guest bring an interesting six-pack of beer (you'll most likely have leftovers, but it will keep for the next party).

Set up a table with a large tub of ice and have everyone place their contribution in the ice when they arrive. Rent beer mugs or buy a box of mason jars for glasses, and chill them directly in the ice.

A double batch of Rockin' Reuben (page 72), a pastrami sandwich on grissini, along with two batches of Pepperoni Pinwheels (page 87), will keep your guests satisfied for two hours. For an additional hour of the party add 36 hors d'oeuvres. Keep it a pub grub–themed menu by adding one batch of 'ZA! (page 58), flavor-packed pizza, or a batch of Sweet Frites (page 65), an innovative twist on beloved french fries. Remember, it's always a good idea to put out a hearty type of pick-up food to supplement the passables—perhaps some nuts and a variety of chips and dips.

a wine revelry

A glass of wine can offer respite from the mundane chores of life and be a call for an occasion. Why not keep a few bottles in stock so that an impromptu party can develop anytime? To be even further prepared, invest in a dozen 10-ounce wine glasses—they can also be used for white wine, mixed drinks, and water.

As you leave the office on a Friday, invite a few colleagues over for a friendly drink to toast the end of the week or to pay tribute to a recent accomplishment. Plan on guests hanging around for three to four hours—after all, it is time to unwind and let loose. And although it seems like a lot, be sure to have at least one bottle of wine per person. If it's a small group and you know their tastes well, you can probably get away with one type of wine. If not, offer a choice between a crowd-pleasing white, like Sauvignon Blanc, and a friendly red, such as Merlot. You can always make it a brown-bag potluck and ask each guest to bring a bottle. Open white wines first and then move on to red. Always keep pitchers or bottles of water nearby for nondrinkers or for pacers between glasses of wine.

Complete the party with hors d'oeuvres that can be prepared fairly quickly—and don't be afraid to let guests help, since the kitchen is a great place to start socializing. For four people, prepare a batch of Little Red Crostini (page 74), a slice of toasted bread topped with red pepper salsa that takes only minutes. For six people, add two batches of nutty-flavored Figs in a Blanket (page 57). For eight people, add one batch of Chickpea Chips (page 85). Keep in mind that an additional cheese platter and some assorted breads are a simple way to satisfy the heartiest of appetites.

a frozen fête

Tropical drinks are the travel agents of cocktails. One sip and you are quickly transported to another place. Glasses overflowing with slushy, frothy drinks adorned with colorful umbrellas and decorative toothpicks are a cause for a fiesta, island style. Gather four friends in your backyard on a warm afternoon to indulge in some rum or tequila concoctions.

If you can find them, purchase fun-shaped plastic disposable glasses, or use large water glasses. If you are feeling extremely festive, cut the centers out of pineapples and use the carved-out rinds as glasses. Don't forget straws. Buy one bottle of liquor and the necessary ingredients for your drink of choice. Measure out the ingredients into a pitcher and pour into the blender as needed along with ice to make drinks to order. Embellish your bar with froufrou stirrers and fruit garnishes.

For a two-hour party, cook up one batch of Uno Mas Quesadillas (page 63) and a batch of Seashells (page 60). The salsa on the quesadillas and the hot chipotle chile in the Seashells are perfect matches for a frozen drink.

figs in a blanket

FRESH FIGS WITH GORGONZOLA AND PROSCIUTTO

This simple yet complex combination of flavors is unbeatable if the figs are perfect. They must be ripe, but not too soft. Try using green as well as purple figs for variety if they are available.

1/2 cup crumbled Gorgonzola

6 small to medium figs, cut into quarters, stems discarded

2 tablespoons balsamic vinegar

2 tablespoons walnut oil (see Note)

1/8 teaspoon kosher salt

1/8 teaspoon pepper

8 ounces prosciutto, thinly sliced, cut into 1 1/2-by-5 1/2-inch strips

Place about 1/2 teaspoon of the Gorgonzola on each fig quarter, pressing gently into the bottom portion of each piece. Place the figs on a parchment paper–lined baking sheet.

Mix the vinegar, oil, kosher salt, and pepper together in a small bowl using a whisk.

to assemble: Brush each fig with the vinegar mixture and wrap the bottom portion with a strip of prosciutto.

do-ahead tip: The figs can be assembled up to 1 hour in advance and covered with plastic wrap. Do not refrigerate.

note: California Press walnut oil, which is available in many specialty food stores, is our favorite. (Or call 707-944-1673 for ordering information.)

yield: 24 FIG QUARTERS

not too strong, not too weak

'ZA!

MINIATURE PIZZAS WITH CAMBOZOLA, ROASTED GARLIC,

SUN-DRIED TOMATOES, AND BASIL

*An English muffin is an ingenious solution for a fast and satisfying pizza crust.
Ready-made roasted garlic can be purchased at some supermarkets and specialty
food stores if you don't have time to roast your own.*

3/4 cup oil-packed sun-dried
tomatoes, strained and julienned

2 teaspoons balsamic vinegar

1/8 teaspoon pepper

4 large heads garlic

2 tablespoons olive oil

6 English muffins, split in half

6 ounces (about 3/4 cup)
Cambozola cheese, at room
temperature

1/4 cup julienned fresh basil

Preheat the oven to 350°F.

Place the sun-dried tomatoes in a small bowl. Add the balsamic
vinegar and season with the pepper. Let marinate.

Cut the top off each head of garlic (make a horizontal cut about 1
inch below the top) and set top back onto head. Place the garlic on a large
piece of aluminum foil and brush with olive oil. Fold the foil to seal the
garlic inside. Bake until the garlic is lightly brown and soft, 50 to 60 minutes. Let cool.

Remove the garlic cloves from the skins by squeezing from the bottom
of each clove. Place in a bowl and mash with the back of a spoon.

to assemble: Increase the oven temperature to 375°F. Spread 1 1/2 teaspoons of garlic over each English muffin. Top each with 1 tablespoon of
Cambozola cheese and 1 tablespoon of sun-dried tomatoes, distributing
evenly over the garlic. Place on a foil- or parchment paper–lined baking
sheet. Bake on the bottom rack of the oven until the cheese melts and the

pizzas become crisp, 10 to 12 minutes. Sprinkle each pizza with the basil and cut into 4 wedges. Serve immediately.

do-ahead tips: The garlic can be roasted and pureed up to 1 week in advance and refrigerated. The pizzas can be assembled up to 3 hours in advance, covered, and left at room temperature until ready to bake. Bake and garnish as directed.

yield: 48 PIZZA WEDGES

not too strong, not too weak

59

seashells

CHIPOTLE–ROCK SHRIMP SALAD WITH CORN
· AND RED PEPPERS IN TORTILLA CUPS

Rock shrimp is wonderful for stuffings and cold salads that are bound with cream cheese or mayonnaise. It is full of flavor and much more economical than the larger shrimp or prawns we know and love. Also, you don't have to peel and devein rock shrimp, which is a real time-saver.

2 tablespoons vegetable oil

³/₄ pound (about 1¹/₂ cups) rock shrimp

¹/₂ teaspoon kosher salt

¹/₈ teaspoon pepper

¹/₂ cup cream cheese, at room temperature

2 tablespoons chopped fresh cilantro

1 tablespoon plus 2 teaspoons lime juice

1 teaspoon minced canned chipotle chiles in adobo sauce (see Note)

¹/₂ teaspoon minced garlic

¹/₂ teaspoon dried oregano

¹/₄ teaspoon onion salt

¹/₂ cup fresh uncooked corn kernels

¹/₃ cup diced red pepper

Three 8-inch flour tortillas

48 cilantro leaves for garnishing

Heat 1 tablespoon of the oil in a large sauté pan over high heat. Season the shrimp with ¹/₄ teaspoon of the kosher salt and the pepper. Sauté over high heat, stirring occasionally, until the shrimp turns pink, 2 to 3 minutes. Transfer to a strainer and let cool. When cool, chop coarsely.

Combine the cream cheese, cilantro, lime juice, chipotle chiles, garlic, oregano, and onion salt in a medium bowl. Stir until well combined. Add the corn, red pepper, and shrimp. Refrigerate until slightly chilled.

Preheat the oven to 350°F.

Place the tortillas in a stack and trim the edges to form a 6-inch square. Brush both sides of each tortilla with the remaining 1 tablespoon oil. Restack the tortillas and cut each into 16 squares.

Press each square firmly into the bottom of miniature (1-inch cup) muffin tins. Season with the remaining $1/4$ teaspoon kosher salt. Bake until golden brown, about 10 minutes. Let cool.

to assemble: Fill each tortilla cup with 1 teaspoon of the shrimp mixture. Garnish with a cilantro leaf and serve.

do-ahead tips: The shrimp salad can be prepared 1 day in advance. The tortilla cups can be prepared up to 5 days in advance and stored in an airtight container. Assemble as directed.

note: Canned chipotle chiles in adobo sauce can be found in super-markets and Latino specialty markets. They can also be purchased by calling Chile-Today and Hot-Tamale, Inc., at 800-468-7377.

yield: 48 FILLED TORTILLA CUPS

not too strong, not too weak

uno mas quesadillas

PEPPER JACK QUESADILLAS WITH TOMATO AND BLACK BEAN SALSA

One of these wickedly rich quesadillas is never enough. They are always devoured as fast as we can serve them. If you're short on time, stop at the store and buy your favorite brand of salsa. While you're there, pick up the makings for margaritas.

SALSA:
- ¾ cup seeded and finely chopped plum tomatoes
- ⅛ teaspoon kosher salt
- ⅓ cup cooked black beans, rinsed and strained
- ¼ cup picante sauce
- 1 tablespoon finely chopped parsley
- 1 tablespoon finely chopped red onion
- 2 teaspoons lime juice
- 1 teaspoon dried oregano
- ½ teaspoon minced fresh garlic

- Eight 6-inch flour tortillas
- 4 ounces pepper jack cheese, grated
- ¼ cup thinly sliced green onions
- Freshly ground pepper
- 3 tablespoons vegetable oil

to make the salsa: Place the tomatoes in a strainer and set over a bowl. Sprinkle with the kosher salt; let sit. Mix the black beans, picante sauce, parsley, red onion, lime juice, oregano and garlic together in a small bowl. Add the tomatoes and stir until incorporated. Refrigerate until ready to use.

Cut the tortillas into 4-inch circles using a 4-inch cutter or a paper template and scissors. Line a baking sheet with half of the tortillas. Divide the cheese and onions evenly among the tortillas on the baking sheet. Season with the pepper. Cover with the remaining tortilla circles and gently press them together.

Heat the oil in a large skillet over medium heat. Add the quesadillas to the skillet and cook until crispy golden brown, about 2 minutes on each side.

(continued)

not too strong, not too weak

Transfer to a paper towel–lined plate. Cut each quesadilla into 8 wedges and top with 1 teaspoon of salsa. Serve immediately.

do-ahead tips: The salsa can be prepared up to 2 days in advance. The quesadillas can be prepared up to 8 hours in advance. Warm in a 400°F oven until crispy, about 10 minutes. Serve as directed.

yield: 32 WEDGES

sweet frites

SWEET POTATO SPEARS WITH SOY-GINGER DIPPING SAUCE

Like most Southerners, we grew up eating sweet potatoes topped with marsh-mallows. These sweet childhood memories fade into the background as this dynamic combination of Asian flavors takes the forefront.

DIPPING SAUCE:

1/3 cup seasoned rice vinegar

1/4 cup soy sauce

1 tablespoon sesame oil

1 teaspoon minced garlic

1 teaspoon grated ginger

1/4 teaspoon red pepper flakes

1 1/2 pounds sweet potatoes, peeled and cut into 3-inch lengths, 1/2 inch thick

2 tablespoons vegetable oil

1/4 teaspoon Chinese five-spice powder

1/4 teaspoon kosher salt

Preheat the oven to 400°F.

to make the dipping sauce: Combine the rice vinegar, soy sauce, sesame oil, garlic, ginger, and red pepper flakes using a whisk. Set aside.

Toss the sweet potatoes in a large bowl with the oil, Chinese five-spice powder, and kosher salt. Bake on a foil- or parchment paper–lined baking sheet until tender, 15 to 20 minutes. Serve immediately with dipping sauce.

do-ahead tips: The dipping sauce can be prepared up to 3 days in advance and refrigerated. The fries can be baked up to 8 hours in advance and reheated in a 400°F oven until warm, about 3 minutes. Serve as directed.

yield: ABOUT 48 FRIES

not too strong, not too weak

noble sword

GRILLED SWORDFISH AND PINEAPPLE ON
SKEWERS WITH GREEN CURRY PESTO

Keep the grill top open when you are cooking these skewers and turn the skewers frequently to prevent them from burning. If there is extra pesto, store it in an airtight container and refrigerate. It adds pizzazz to ordinary steamed rice or pasta.

PESTO:

1/2 cup macadamia nuts

1/2 cup firmly packed fresh cilantro leaves

1/2 cup firmly packed fresh mint leaves

3 tablespoons olive oil

2 tablespoons sweetened shredded coconut

2 teaspoons lime juice

1 teaspoon fish sauce (see Note, page 49)

3/4 teaspoon green curry paste (see Note, page 51)

1/2 teaspoon minced fresh garlic

1 1/4 pounds swordfish, cut into 3/4-inch cubes

2 tablespoons vegetable oil

3/4 teaspoon kosher salt

1/4 teaspoon pepper

1/2 fresh pineapple, cut into 3/4-inch pieces

36 five-inch bamboo skewers (see Note)

Preheat grill to medium heat.

to make the pesto: Mix the nuts, cilantro, mint, olive oil, coconut, lime juice, fish sauce, curry paste, and garlic together in a food processor. Process until the nuts are finely chopped and the mixture is well combined.

Toss the swordfish with 1 tablespoon of the vegetable oil, 1/2 teaspoon of the kosher salt, and the pepper in a medium bowl. Toss the pineapple with the remaining 1 tablespoon vegetable oil and remaining 1/4 teaspoon kosher salt in a separate bowl. Slide 1 piece of pineapple onto a skewer.

66

Follow with 1 piece of swordfish. Repeat until all of the ingredients have been used. Place the skewers on the grill and cook until the fish is opaque in the center, 6 to 8 minutes on each side. Turn frequently.

Spoon $^1/_2$ teaspoon of the pesto over each skewer and serve warm.

do-ahead tips: The pesto can be prepared up to 2 days in advance and refrigerated. The skewers can be grilled 1 day in advance and refrigerated. Wrap in foil and tightly seal the edges before warming slightly in a 300°F oven for 5 to 7 minutes. Serve as directed.

note: Soak the bamboo skewers in water for at least fifteen minutes before using to prevent splintering and burning.

yield: ABOUT 36 SKEWERS

not too strong, not too weak

vietnamese wrapture

GROUND PORK WITH HOISIN, MINT, AND BASIL WRAPPED IN RICE PAPER

Rice paper actually comes from the appropriately named rice-paper plant or tree. But sometimes it is made with rice flour. It is a very delicate, thin sheet that needs to be reconstituted in water before being used. It may take a little patience to work with at first but the results are well worth it. Keep a few extra sheets on hand in case of tearing. Look for rice paper at supermarkets and in Asian specialty food stores.

12 ounces ground pork

$1/4$ teaspoon kosher salt

$1/4$ teaspoon pepper

$1/2$ cup hoisin sauce

One 8-ounce can water chestnuts, strained and coarsely chopped

$1/3$ cup chopped green onions, green part only

24 six-inch round sheets rice paper (have a few extra on hand in case of tearing)

1 tablespoon black sesame seeds

24 medium basil leaves

24 medium mint leaves

Heat the pork in a large nonstick skillet over high heat. Season with the salt and pepper. Cook until the meat is no longer pink, about 5 minutes, stirring frequently. Transfer the pork to a paper towel–lined plate using a slotted spoon. Let cool.

Mix the hoisin sauce, water chestnuts, and green onions together in a small bowl. Add the pork and mix well. Refrigerate while preparing the rice papers.

to assemble: Fill a pie plate or other wide, shallow container with lukewarm water (do not use cold water or hot water). Place 2 rice papers in the water. Let sit until somewhat soft, about 45 seconds. Remove 1 paper at a time and place on a paper towel. Cover with an additional paper towel. Repeat the process until there are 12 layers of rice paper. The rice

(continued)

paper will become pliable 1 to 2 minutes after being stacked. Invert the stack and use the rice papers in the order in which they were removed from the water.

Place 3 rice papers at a time on a clean work surface. Sprinkle each rice paper with $^1/_8$ teaspoon of the sesame seeds. Place 1 basil leaf on the bottom third of each rice paper. Top with 1 tablespoon of the pork mixture. Cover with 1 mint leaf. Fold the right and left edges toward the center of the filling, pressing firmly. Fold the bottom edge of the rice paper toward the center and gently but firmly roll until the top edge is reached and a rectangle $1^1/_2$ by 2 inches is formed. Repeat until the first 12 rice paper rolls are complete. Cover assembled wraps with a very damp towel and cover with plastic wrap. Soak remaining rice paper wraps and assemble until remaining ingredients have been used. Cover the wraps as directed. These rolls can be left at room temperature for up to 3 hours. Do not refrigerate or the rice papers will harden.

do-ahead tip: The pork mixture can be prepared up to 1 day in advance and refrigerated.

yield: 24 RICE-PAPER ROLLS

peanut plantation

FRIED PLANTAINS WITH PEANUT SALSA

Our grandfather was a peanut processor in Suffolk, Virginia. He would be proud to taste this innovative and unusual concoction. Serve this hors d'oeuvre with piña coladas and your guests will feel like they have been transported to the Caribbean, where plantains are a mainstay in the cuisine.

5 tablespoons chopped green onions, green part only

2 tablespoons sesame oil

1 tablespoon honey

2 teaspoons lime juice

1 teaspoon grated peeled fresh ginger

$3/4$ cup unsalted roasted peanuts

2 tablespoons peanut oil

3 medium-ripe plantains (should be soft to the touch), peeled and cut on the diagonal into $1/2$-inch-thick slices

$1/2$ teaspoon kosher salt

Mix 3 tablespoons of the green onions, sesame oil, honey, lime juice, and ginger together in a small bowl.

Chop the peanuts finely using a food processor. Add the green onion mixture and pulse once or twice just until mixed. Do not overprocess. Transfer to a bowl, cover, and serve within 3 hours. Do not refrigerate.

Heat the peanut oil in a large sauté pan over medium heat. Season both sides of the plantains with the kosher salt. Sauté until golden brown, about 2 minutes per side. Transfer to a paper towel–lined baking sheet to absorb any extra oil.

to assemble: Place 1 teaspoon of the peanut salsa on each plantain. Garnish with the remaining 2 tablespoons of green onions and serve.

do-ahead tip: The plantains can be sautéed up to 3 hours in advance and reheated in a 400°F oven until warm. Do not refrigerate. Assemble as directed.

yield: ABOUT 24 PLANTAINS

not too strong, not too weak

rockin' reuben

Grissini *is the Italian word for breadsticks. Authentic* grissini *are very thin, making them perfect for this recipe. Look for them in the cracker or bread section of supermarkets, or buy them at an Italian delicatessen or bakery.*

DIPPING SAUCE:

1/2 cup mayonnaise

1/4 cup plus 1 tablespoon ketchup

2 tablespoons strained
    sauerkraut, chopped

1/2 teaspoon caraway seeds

1/2 pound thinly sliced pastrami,
    cut into 1 1/2-by-6-inch strips

24 arugula leaves, stems
    removed

8 to 12 very thin (about 1/2 inch
    thick) breadsticks, cut into
    4-inch lengths

to make the dipping sauce: Mix the mayonnaise, ketchup, sauerkraut, and caraway seeds together in a small bowl using a whisk. Set aside.

Spread the pastrami on a work surface and cover each strip with a slightly larger arugula leaf. Roll each arugula-covered pastrami strip tightly around the end of each breadstick and place seam-side down. Serve with the dipping sauce.

do-ahead tips: The dipping sauce can be prepared up to 3 days in advance and refrigerated. The breadsticks can be assembled up to 1 hour in advance, covered with plastic wrap, and refrigerated.

yield: 24 WRAPPED BREADSTICKS

little red crostini

TOASTED BREAD SLICES TOPPED WITH ROASTED RED PEPPER SALSA

Most baguette slices are dangerously big for a cocktail party. Avoid embarrassing spills by cutting large slices in half. Even your "big-mouth" friends will appreciate the gesture! Fines herbes is a classic blend of dried herbs that includes tarragon, parsley, chervil, and chives. If it isn't available in a supermarket near you, substitute herbes de Provence.

1 French baguette, cut into twenty-four 1/4-inch-thick slices (if the slices are bigger than 1 1/2 inches in diameter, cut them in half)

1 1/2 teaspoons fines herbes (see recipe introduction)

1/2 teaspoon kosher salt

1/4 teaspoon plus 1 pinch pepper

1/4 cup olive oil

SALSA:

1 cup finely chopped onions

One 7-ounce jar roasted red peppers, strained well, coarsely chopped

2 tablespoons chopped fresh basil

1 tablespoon capers, strained

1 tablespoon chopped fresh parsley

2 teaspoons extra-virgin olive oil

2 teaspoons balsamic vinegar

1/2 teaspoon minced garlic

1/4 teaspoon kosher salt

Preheat the oven to 350°F.

Arrange the bread on a baking sheet. Mix the fines herbes, 1/4 teaspoon of the kosher salt, and 1/4 teaspoon of the pepper in a small bowl. Add 3 tablespoons of the olive oil and mix well. Brush the herb mixture over the bread. Bake until crisp and golden brown, 10 to 12 minutes. Check to see that the bread is cooking evenly; if necessary turn the baking sheet around in the oven.

to make the salsa: Heat remaining 1 tablespoon olive oil in a medium nonstick skillet over medium heat. Add the onions. Season with remaining $^1/_4$ teaspoon of the kosher salt and a pinch of pepper. Cook until the onions are tender, about 5 minutes. Remove from heat.

Mix the onions, red peppers, basil, capers, parsley, 2 teaspoons olive oil, vinegar, garlic, and kosher salt. Refrigerate until chilled.

to assemble: Place 1 heaping teaspoon of the red-pepper mixture on each crostini.

do-ahead tips: The crostini can be prepared up to 5 days in advance and stored in an airtight container. The red-pepper mixture can be prepared up to 1 day in advance. Assemble up to 1 hour in advance.

yield: ABOUT 48 TOPPED CROSTINI

not too strong, not too weak

strata frittata

BAKED EGGS WITH HAM AND SWISS CHEESE

These delectable little squares have qualities of both a strata and a frittata. This recipe is similar to a strata in that it is, in essence, a one-dish egg casserole with the addition of bread. We have reduced the amount of bread that links this recipe to the frittata, a cooked egg dish that resembles an omelette. At any rate, you say strata, we say frittata . . . both words loosely describe this rustic source of comfort food.

Butter for baking dish

Flour for baking dish

1 tablespoon bacon grease or olive oil

1 1/2 cups finely chopped onions

1/4 teaspoon kosher salt

1/4 teaspoon pepper

5 large eggs

1 cup (about 6 ounces) chopped ham

3/4 cup grated Swiss cheese

1/3 cup cream

1/4 cup dried bread crumbs

3 tablespoons chopped fresh chives

1 teaspoon chopped fresh rosemary

3/4 teaspoon chopped dried sage

Preheat the oven to 325°F.

Coat the sides and bottom of an 8-by-8-by-2 1/2-inch glass baking dish with butter and flour.

Heat the bacon grease in a medium nonstick skillet over medium heat. Add the onions and season with the kosher salt and 1/8 teaspoon of the pepper. Cook the onions until tender, 8 to 10 minutes.

Beat the eggs in a medium bowl. Add the onions, ham, cheese, cream, bread crumbs, 2 tablespoons of the chives, rosemary, sage, and the remaining 1/8 teaspoon pepper and stir to mix well.

Pour the egg mixture into the prepared dish and sprinkle the remaining 1 tablespoon chives over the top. Bake until the mixture has set (is firm in

(continued)

the center), 35 to 45 minutes. Place on a rack to cool. Trim the outside edges. Cut into 25 squares. Place on a baking sheet and cover with foil. Reheat for about 5 minutes before serving.

do-ahead tip: The egg mixture can be baked up to 2 days in advance and refrigerated, or frozen up to 1 week in advance. Let thaw. Cut and warm as directed.

yield: 25 SQUARES

dab a crab

CRAB AND CORN SALAD ON HOMEMADE CORN CHIPS

You'll say "adios" to plain old chips and salsa after you taste one bite of this dynamite combination of flavors. This lowfat baked tortilla chip hits the spot when topped with a dab of Latin-inspired crab and corn salad.

1/4 cup cream cheese, at room temperature

1/4 cup sliced green onions

2 tablespoons mayonnaise

2 tablespoons lemon juice

1 teaspoon ground cumin

1/2 teaspoon kosher salt

1/8 teaspoon pepper

6 ounces fresh crabmeat, picked over for shells, well strained

1/2 cup fresh uncooked corn kernels

Six 6 1/2-inch corn tortillas

2 tablespoons vegetable oil

48 cilantro leaves for garnishing

Combine the cream cheese, green onions, mayonnaise, lemon juice, cumin, 1/4 teaspoon of the kosher salt, and pepper in a small bowl. Stir in the crabmeat and corn. Refrigerate until ready to serve.

Preheat the oven to 400°F.

Place the tortillas in a stack and trim the edges to form a 5-inch square. Brush both sides of each tortilla with the oil. Restack the tortillas and cut them into 4 squares. Cut each square in half diagonally to make triangles.

Arrange the tortillas on baking sheets. Season with the remaining 1/4 teaspoon kosher salt. Bake until golden brown, 10 to 15 minutes. Let cool.

to assemble: Top each chip with 1 teaspoon of the crab mixture. Garnish with a cilantro leaf and serve.

do-ahead tips: The crab mixture can be prepared up to 1 day in advance and refrigerated. The tortilla chips can be prepared up to 1 day in advance and stored in an airtight container.

yield: 48 TOPPED CHIPS

sinful spuds

NEW POTATOES STUFFED WITH FETA, GREEN OLIVES, AND PINE NUTS

The combination of feta, olives, and pine nuts nestled in a potato is divine. For a creative presentation, cut a lemon in half and use it as an oasis for a fresh herb bouquet (cut a thin slice off the bottom so it will lie flat). Rosemary and thyme work well because they don't wilt.

12 small new potatoes, uniform in size and shape

6 cups water

1 1/2 teaspoons kosher salt

1/2 cup feta

1/4 cup toasted pine nuts

2 tablespoons chopped green olives

1 tablespoon extra-virgin olive oil

1 tablespoon dried currants

1/2 teaspoon chopped lemon zest

1/4 teaspoon oregano

1/4 teaspoon pepper

24 parsley leaves for garnishing

Cut a thin slice off the top and bottom of each potato. Cut the potatoes in half crosswise. Place in a large saucepan and cover with the water. Add the kosher salt. Bring to a boil over high heat. Reduce the heat and let simmer. Cook until the potatoes are tender when pierced with a fork, 10 to 15 minutes. Be careful not to overcook. Strain and let cool.

Crumble the feta with a fork in a small bowl. Add the pine nuts, green olives, olive oil, currants, lemon zest, oregano, and pepper. Mix well.

to assemble: Scoop out the center of each potato with a spoon or melon baller. Fill the centers with a heaping teaspoon of the feta mixture. Garnish with a parsley leaf.

do-ahead tips: The feta mixture can be prepared up to 2 days in advance and refrigerated. (Do not add the pine nuts until ready to assemble, and let the mixture sit at room temperature 1 hour before assembly.) The potatoes can be assembled up to 4 hours in advance.

yield: 24 FILLED POTATOES

turk-n-roll

When tortillas are baked they become crispy like a piecrust. Wrapped around a savory smoked turkey filling, they make an outstanding hors d'oeuvre. Serve these hot sensations on a plate garnished with colorful fresh chiles. Complete the party with sangria and salsa music.

DIPPING SAUCE:

3/4 cup sour cream

3 tablespoons chopped fresh cilantro

2 teaspoons concentrated mole (see Note)

1 1/2 teaspoons fresh lime juice

1/4 teaspoon kosher salt

1/2 cup (about 1/4 pound, thinly sliced) finely chopped smoked turkey

1/4 cup canned diced green chiles

1 teaspoon minced garlic

1/2 teaspoon dried oregano

1 tablespoon concentrated mole

Six 7-inch fresh flour tortillas, unrefrigerated

Vegetable oil for brushing the tortillas

to make the dipping sauce: Combine the sour cream, cilantro, 2 teaspoons mole, lime juice, and kosher salt in a small bowl using a whisk. Refrigerate until chilled.

Mix the turkey, chiles, garlic, oregano, and 1 tablespoon mole together in a small bowl. Mix well.

Preheat the oven to 400°F.

Cut each tortilla into four 2 1/2-inch circles using a cookie cutter or paper template and scissors. Lay the tortillas, 6 at a time, on a work surface. Brush lightly with the vegetable oil. Place 1 teaspoon of the turkey mixture on the lower third of each tortilla. Roll up tightly and secure by pushing a toothpick all the way through the roll. Place the tortillas on a parchment paper–lined baking sheet. Brush each tortilla lightly with oil. Bake until light brown, 10 to 12 minutes. Remove toothpicks and serve with the dipping sauce.

do-ahead tips: The dipping sauce can be prepared up to 2 days in advance. The tortillas can be baked up to 1 day in advance and refrigerated. Warm in a 350°F oven before serving.

note: Look for concentrated mole in a jar at supermarkets or Latin specialty shops. The brand we like best is Embassa. Don't be alarmed if the oil separates and gathers at the top, just stir until it is incorporated.

yield: 24 TORTILLA ROLL-UPS

not too strong, not too weak

chickpea chips

PAPRIKA CHIPS WITH HUMMUS

Chickpeas, often called garbanzo or ceci beans, are sweet little beans that puree beautifully to create a creamy dip. If you don't have time to make your own hummus, buy some at a deli or specialty store and use it on top of these tasty, crunchy chips. No one will ever know that you didn't make it yourself.

$1^1/_2$ teaspoons ground cumin

$^3/_4$ teaspoon sweet paprika

$^1/_4$ teaspoon plus $^1/_8$ teaspoon kosher salt

2 tablespoons vegetable oil

4 miniature (4 inches in diameter) pocket pitas

One 15-ounce can plus one $8^3/_4$-ounce can chickpeas, drained

$^1/_4$ cup tahini

3 tablespoons water

2 tablespoons lemon juice

2 teaspoons extra-virgin olive oil

1 teaspoon ground coriander

$^1/_2$ teaspoon minced garlic

$^1/_8$ teaspoon cayenne

48 cilantro sprigs for garnishing

Preheat the oven to 350°F.

Mix $^1/_2$ teaspoon of the cumin, paprika, and $^1/_8$ teaspoon of the kosher salt together in a small bowl. Add the oil and mix well. Cut the edges off the pitas, using scissors, and separate into 2 pieces. Brush the rough side of each piece of pita with the oil. Stack the pita and cut into six wedges. Arrange the wedges on a parchment paper–lined baking sheet, seasoned-side up. Bake on the middle rack of the oven until crisp and golden, 8 to 10 minutes.

to make the hummus: Place the 15-ounce can of chickpeas into a food processor. Add the tahini, water, lemon juice, olive oil, coriander, garlic, cayenne, remaining 1 teaspoon cumin, and $^1/_4$ teaspoon kosher salt in a food processor and process until smooth.

(continued)

not too strong, not too weak

to assemble: Transfer the hummus to a sealable plastic bag and squeeze into one corner. Cut a small tip off the corner. Pipe about 1 teaspoon onto each pita wedge. Garnish with a cilantro sprig and a whole chickpea.

do-ahead tips: The chips can be baked up to 3 days in advance and stored in an airtight container. The hummus can be prepared up to 2 days in advance and refrigerated. The chips can be assembled up to 30 minutes in advance.

yield: 48 CHIPS

pepperoni pinwheels

PUFF PASTRY WITH PEPPERONI, GRUYÈRE, AND HONEY MUSTARD

The first time we made these, we tried one and it was all over. We lost all restraint and devoured the entire batch while hovering over the stove. These are so light and flaky they inspire gluttony, so always double or triple this recipe or you'll be sorry!

½ cup finely grated Gruyère cheese

¾ teaspoon dried sage

¾ teaspoon dried oregano

¼ teaspoon pepper

1 puff pastry sheet, thawed

2 tablespoons honey mustard

2 ounces packaged sliced pepperoni

1 egg, lightly beaten

Mix the Gruyère, sage, oregano, and pepper together in a small bowl. Lay the puff pastry on a lightly floured surface with a short side closest to you. Cut in half crosswise. Arrange a long side closest to you. Divide the mustard and spread evenly over the sheets of puff pastry, leaving a 1-inch border at the top edge. Divide the pepperoni and arrange in a single layer over the mustard. Top with the Gruyère mixture. Brush the farthest edge of each half with the egg. Roll the puff pastry tightly from the closest edge toward the egg-coated edge. Lay, seam-side down, on a baking sheet and chill until firm, about 30 minutes.

Preheat the oven to 400°F.

Cut the logs into ¼-inch-thick slices and arrange, cut-side down, 1 inch apart on a foil- or parchment paper–lined baking sheet. Bake, one baking sheet at a time, in the middle of the oven until golden, about 14 minutes. Serve warm.

do-ahead tip: The puff pastry can be filled and rolled up to 1 day in advance and refrigerated, or frozen up to 2 weeks in advance. Thaw, cut, and bake as directed.

yield: 48 PINWHEELS

not too strong, not too weak

get figgy

CORNBREAD WITH FIG TAPENADE

The secret to these hors d'oeuvres is to serve them warm, because the flavors of the tapenade are emphasized and the texture of the cornbread becomes soft and ethereal. To create a striking presentation, arrange these golden bites on a dark plate. The colors will really pop and make it as enticing to look at as it is to eat.

Vegetable oil for the baking dish

1 1/4 cups cornmeal

3/4 cup all-purpose flour

2 teaspoons baking powder

1 1/2 teaspoons kosher salt

4 tablespoons (1/2 stick) chilled unsalted butter, cut into pea-size pieces

2 large eggs, separated

1 1/2 cups heavy cream

3 tablespoons honey

1 1/2 cups finely chopped dried figs, stems removed

1/2 cup plus 2 tablespoons water

1/2 cup kalamata olives, pitted and chopped

1/3 cup pine nuts, toasted

2 tablespoons balsamic vinegar

2 tablespoons extra-virgin olive oil

2 tablespoons strained capers, chopped

2 teaspoons chopped fresh thyme

1/4 teaspoon pepper

Chives cut into 1-inch pieces for garnishing, optional

Preheat the oven to 400°F.

Brush a 9-by-13-inch baking dish with the vegetable oil. Put the cornmeal, flour, baking powder, and kosher salt in a food processor. Pulse to mix. Add the butter and pulse until the mixture resembles coarse cornmeal. Transfer to a large bowl.

Combine the egg yolks, cream, and honey in medium bowl using a whisk. Add to the dry ingredients, stirring constantly. Beat the egg whites in a small bowl until stiff but not dry. Fold half of the egg whites into the cornmeal mixture; fold in the remaining egg whites. Spoon the batter into the prepared baking dish. Bake until a tester inserted into the center comes out clean, about 15 minutes. Transfer to a wire rack and cool slightly. Reduce the oven to 350°F.

Mix the figs and water together in a small saucepan set over medium heat. Cook until the liquid evaporates and the figs are very soft, about 7 minutes. Transfer to a small bowl. Add the olives, pine nuts, vinegar, olive oil, capers, thyme, and pepper. Mix well.

to assemble: Trim the brown edges from the cornbread and cut into 1-inch squares. Top each square with 1 teaspoon of the fig tapenade. Place on a baking sheet, cover with foil, and bake until warm, about 5 minutes. If desired, arrange 2 chives in a crisscross design on the top before serving.

do-ahead tips: The fig tapenade can be prepared, except for the pine nuts, up to 3 days in advance (add the pine nuts just prior to serving). The cornbread can be baked up to 1 day in advance. Assemble up to 2 hours in advance with the fig tapenade and bake according to directions. Garnish with chives just prior to serving.

yield: 60 CORNBREAD SQUARES

not too strong, not too weak

polenta sunrise

POLENTA WITH SUN-DRIED TOMATO SALSA

After cooking numerous batches of polenta during our restaurant days and, we might add, after burning more than a batch or two, we learned an invaluable tip. During the final stages of cooking the polenta, we like to alternate between a whisk and a plastic spatula. The whisk helps prevent lumps and the plastic spatula, dragged evenly and firmly against the bottom of the pan, helps prevent sticking. With this simple technique, you won't have to fret about your polenta burning.

Vegetable oil for coating the baking dish

2 3/4 cups water

3/4 teaspoon kosher salt

1/2 cup polenta

1/3 cup heavy cream

1/2 cup Parmesan cheese

SALSA:

1 1/4 cups drained, julienned oil-packed sun-dried tomatoes

3 tablespoons chopped fresh basil

1 tablespoon balsamic vinegar

3/4 teaspoon minced garlic

1/8 teaspoon pepper

Brush an 8-by-8-by-2 1/2-inch glass baking dish with the oil. Bring the water and kosher salt to a boil in a heavy, medium saucepan over medium heat. Add the polenta using a whisk to incorporate. Reduce the heat. Let simmer for about 10 minutes, stirring frequently. Add the cream, using a whisk to incorporate. Cook until the consistency is soft and thick, about 10 minutes. Remove from the heat and add the Parmesan cheese, using a whisk to incorporate. Pour the polenta into the prepared baking dish and spread evenly into the dish using a large spatula or the back of a large spoon. Refrigerate until chilled.

to make the salsa: Mix the sun-dried tomatoes, basil, balsamic vinegar, garlic, and pepper together in a small bowl.

(continued)

not too strong, not too weak

to assemble: Preheat the oven to 300°F. Trim the edges of the polenta and cut into 36 squares. Top each square with $^1/_2$ teaspoon of the salsa. Place on a foil- or parchment paper-lined baking sheet. Bake until slightly warm, 8 to 10 minutes. Serve warm.

do-ahead tips: The polenta and the salsa can be prepared up to 2 days in advance. The squares can be assembled up to 1 day in advance. Bake as directed.

yield: 36 POLENTA SQUARES

artichoke truffles

ARTICHOKE HEARTS WITH GOAT CHEESE, TARRAGON, AND PARMESAN

These fabulous little taste sensations are at their best when served slightly chilled. Serve them in a decorative bowl or cover a plate with whole flat-leaf parsley leaves and set the bites on top.

3/4 cup freshly grated Parmesan

2 tablespoons chopped parsley

4 ounces cream cheese, at room temperature

3 ounces goat cheese, at room temperature

2 teaspoons grated lemon zest or 3 drops lemon oil

1 teaspoon dried tarragon

1/8 teaspoon pepper

two 6 1/2-ounce jars marinated artichoke hearts, strained and trimmed to uniform bite-sized pieces, about 1 1/2 inches by 3/4 inches

Mix the Parmesan and parsley together in a small bowl. Combine the cream cheese, goat cheese, lemon zest, tarragon, and pepper in a medium bowl. Add the artichokes and mix to coat each heart liberally. Transfer to the bowl of Parmesan and roll to cover completely. Place on a parchment or waxed paper–lined baking sheet. Refrigerate until firm, about 1 hour. Let sit at room temperature for 30 minutes before serving.

do-ahead tips: The cream cheese mixture can be prepared and refrigerated up to 3 days in advance and brought back to room temperature before coating the artichokes. The artichoke truffles can be assembled up to 1 day in advance and refrigerated.

yield: ABOUT 24 TRUFFLES

not too strong, not too weak

light and delicate

an array of subtle yet scrumptious finger foods to pair with beverages of finesse

GRACEFUL SCALLOPS, SEXY ASPARAGUS, CURVACEOUS TOMATOES, TOOTHSOME goat cheese, and elegant artichoke leaves: this chapter is filled with sensuous ingredients waiting to be paired with gracious libations, so pop a few corks or unleash a liqueur with these indulgent finger foods. Your guests will be stirred by such sensational marriages of good taste.

Celebrate life's little pleasures with a Sparkling Endeavor or an Aperitif Affair:

a sparkling endeavor

Nothing signals a special occasion more than a glass of bubbly. Pull out all the stops to honor a momentous event in life: an engagement, a promotion, a new baby, or a goal attained.

For a large celebration with a guest list of twenty, purchase one case of champagne or sparkling wine (always purchase one bottle in advance before making a large purchase, tasting it to be sure it's to your liking). Don't forget the champagne flutes (the round bowl glasses cause champagne to lose its bubbles quickly), a decorative ice bucket, and a silver tray.

At least thirty minutes before your guests arrive, place the champagne in a large cooler chest filled with ice and water (hide this in the kitchen or under a cloth-covered table). Reserve a few bottles; they can be added later if needed or stored for a future celebration. Add a few bottles of sparkling water to the mix. Place two to three bottles in an ice- and water-filled decorative ice bucket for easy access. Set your glasses on a silver tray and, as guests arrive, greet them with the tray of filled glasses.

For a three-hour party, prepare two batches of Tuna Tied (page 103), delectable bites of tuna decorated with a scallion ribbon and complemented by the essence of oranges; add two batches of Chix Stix (page 113). Include two recipes of Rosemary's Tartlets (page 119), impressive bite-sized tarts filled with a sweet and savory mixture of grapes, walnuts, and Brie cheese. As the crowning touch, treat your guests to a couple batches of Leaves of Glory (page 107), a glorious combination of basil and Parmesan set atop individual artichoke leaves. Note that it is a good idea to offer a couple more substantial "grazing" items such as a smoked salmon and pumpernickel platter with cream cheese and dill, and a caviar display with all the fixings.

an aperitif affair

Plan an intimate gathering of four or six. Buy one or two bottles of a liqueur such as Campari or Lillet. Fill a decorative bowl or ice bucket with ice cubes and lay out a pair of ice tongs. Set out the proper number of glasses, plus a couple of extras. Offer bottles of soda water or a pitcher of water, should anyone want to dilute their drink.

Complete your evening with a batch of Caprese Skewers (page 101), a medley of fresh tomatoes and mozzarella cheese. Surprise your guests with a batch of Shrimply Delish (page 117), a thoroughly modern shrimp cocktail. And round out the menu with a recipe for Red, Hot, and Cool (page 105).

focaccia fantastico

FOCACCIA WITH CARAMELIZED CITRUS ONIONS,
GOAT CHEESE, AND ASPARAGUS

Focaccia is an Italian flatbread that is made with olive oil. It is "molto bene" when topped with this combination of sweet onion confit, creamy goat cheese, and crisp asparagus. Look for focaccia bread in supermarkets and at Italian specialty shops or bakeries. Complete your menu with a glass of Pinot Grigio or Sangiovese.

2 tablespoons olive oil

3 cups finely chopped onions

1 teaspoon plus 1 pinch kosher salt

$^1/_4$ teaspoon plus 1 pinch white pepper

$^1/_4$ cup orange juice concentrate

2 tablespoons lemon juice

2 tablespoons champagne vinegar

1 tablespoon plus 1 teaspoon lime juice

1 tablespoon plus 1 teaspoon lemon zest

2 teaspoons dried tarragon

$^1/_4$ cup goat cheese, at room temperature

$^1/_4$ cup cream cheese, at room temperature

$^1/_4$ cup grated Parmesan cheese

48 (about 2 bunches) asparagus tips, cut into 1$^1/_2$-inch lengths, blanched

1 tablespoon plus 1 teaspoon extra-virgin olive oil

One 10-by-8-inch piece of focaccia, cut into 1$^1/_4$-inch squares

Heat the olive oil in a large nonstick skillet over medium heat. Add the onions and season with 1 teaspoon of the kosher salt and $^1/_4$ teaspoon of the white pepper. Cook the onions until translucent, about 15 minutes. Do not let brown. Mix the orange juice concentrate, lemon juice, vinegar, lime juice, lemon zest, and tarragon together in a small bowl. Add the orange juice mixture to the onions and cook until the liquid is absorbed and the onions are soft and sweet, 12 to 15 minutes. Transfer to a small bowl and let cool.

Cream together the goat cheese, cream cheese, and Parmesan cheese in a small bowl. Put the asparagus in a small bowl and drizzle with 1 teaspoon of the extra-virgin olive oil; toss to coat well. Season with the remaining pinch of kosher salt and remaining pinch of white pepper.

Preheat the oven to 375°F.

to assemble: Brush the focaccia lightly with the remaining 1 tablespoon extra-virgin olive oil. Top each square with $^1/_2$ teaspoon of the cheese mixture, 1 teaspoon of the onions, and 1 asparagus tip. Bake until warm, 3 to 5 minutes.

do-ahead tips: The onions can be prepared up to 3 days in advance and refrigerated. The cheese mixture can be prepared up to 3 days in advance and refrigerated. The squares can be assembled up to 4 hours in advance. Bake as directed.

yield: 48 SQUARES

spear ecstasy

ASPARAGUS WITH LEMON-TARRAGON DIPPING SAUCE

Arrange the asparagus spears in beautiful crystal glasses or silver cups and pour the sauce into a matching glass. This dish is best when the dipping sauce and asparagus are served chilled, so allow time to refrigerate.

DIPPING SAUCE:

3/4 cup sour cream

1/4 cup mayonnaise

3 tablespoons chopped red onion

2 tablespoons lemon juice

1 tablespoon plus 1 teaspoon capers, drained and chopped

2 teaspoons chopped lemon zest

2 teaspoons dried tarragon

1/2 teaspoon onion powder

1/2 teaspoon sugar

1/4 teaspoon pepper

48 (about 2 bunches) asparagus spears, cut into 4-inch lengths

3 cups ice

6 cups water

1 1/2 teaspoons kosher salt

to make the dipping sauce: Mix the sour cream, mayonnaise, onion, lemon juice, capers, lemon zest, tarragon, onion powder, sugar, and pepper together using a whisk. Mix well. Refrigerate until chilled, about 2 hours.

Cook the asparagus in a steamer basket over boiling water until tender when pierced with a fork, 6 to 8 minutes. Mix the ice, water, and kosher salt together in a large bowl. Remove the asparagus from the steamer and refresh it by plunging it into the ice water. Let sit until cold. Transfer to a paper towel–lined plate to dry. Refrigerate. Serve chilled with the dipping sauce.

do-ahead tips: The dipping sauce can be prepared up to 2 days in advance and refrigerated. The asparagus can be prepared 1 day in advance and refrigerated. Serve as directed.

yield: 48 ASPARAGUS SPEARS

light and delicate

caprese skewers

CHERRY TOMATO, MOZZARELLA, AND BASIL SKEWERS

The lineup of red tomato, white mozzarella, and green basil makes these skewers an optical treat. Savor these during the summer when tomatoes are at their peak. Alternate the red cherry tomatoes with yellow pear tomatoes.

1 tablespoon balsamic vinegar

1 tablespoon plus 1 teaspoon extra-virgin olive oil

1/4 teaspoon pepper

1/8 teaspoon kosher salt, plus more for seasoning

4 ounces mozzarella cheese, cut into twenty-four 1/2-inch cubes (fresh mozzarella is best)

24 small (or 12 large, cut in half) cherry tomatoes, preferably Sweet 100s

24 small to medium fresh basil leaves

24 five-inch bamboo skewers (see Note, page 104)

Combine the balsamic vinegar, 1 tablespoon of the olive oil, 1/8 teaspoon of the pepper, and 1/8 teaspoon of the kosher salt in a small bowl using a whisk. Set aside.

Toss the mozzarella with the remaining 1 teaspoon olive oil and the remaining pepper. Season to taste with kosher salt, if necessary, depending on the taste of the mozzarella.

to assemble: Slide 1 cherry tomato onto a skewer. Fold 1 basil leaf in half; slide onto the skewer. Add 1 piece of mozzarella. Repeat until all of the ingredients have been used. Place skewers on a plate and brush with the balsamic vinaigrette. Transfer to a platter and serve immediately.

do-ahead tips: The balsamic vinaigrette can be prepared 3 days in advance and refrigerated. Assemble the skewers and cover with plastic wrap up to 3 hours in advance. Do not refrigerate. Serve as directed.

yield: 24 SKEWERS

light and delicate

tuna tied

SCALLION-WRAPPED TUNA WITH ORANGE-MISO DIPPING SAUCE

We have served this hors d'oeuvre to several of our friends who claim to hate miso. Boy, have they been fooled. We waited until the platter was empty to tell them about the secret ingredient. Now they request the orange-miso dipping sauce with other fish dishes, as a salad dressing, and as a dip for crudités. It's also delicious with chicken.

DIPPING SAUCE:
- 3 tablespoons orange juice concentrate
- 2 tablespoons shiro miso (see Note)
- 1 teaspoon lime juice
- 1/4 cup sesame oil
- 3 tablespoons vegetable oil

- 36 (about 2 bunches) green onions, green part only, trimmed to 5-inch lengths
- 1 1/4 pounds sashimi-quality tuna, cut into thirty-six 3/4-inch cubes
- 1 tablespoon vegetable oil
- 1/2 teaspoon kosher salt, plus more for salted ice water
- 1/4 teaspoon pepper
- 36 five-inch bamboo skewers (see Note)

to make the dipping sauce: Combine the orange juice concentrate, miso, and lime juice in a small bowl using a whisk. Add the sesame oil and vegetable oil in a slow, steady stream, whisking constantly. Refrigerate until chilled.

Bring a small saucepan of salted water to a boil. Add the green onions and cook until wilted and bright green, about 45 seconds. Immediately plunge into salted ice water until cool. Strain and transfer to a paper towel–lined plate to dry.

Preheat the grill to high.

Mix the tuna with the vegetable oil, kosher salt, and pepper in a medium bowl. Toss to coat well. Grill until the exterior begins to cook but the center is still rare, about 3 minutes, turning at least once.

(continued)

to assemble: Preheat the oven to 350°F. Wrap a scallion around 1 piece of tuna and secure it with a skewer. Repeat until all of the ingredients have been used. Wrap the skewers in foil and seal the edges. Bake until slightly warm, about 5 minutes. Serve with the dipping sauce.

do-ahead tips: The dipping sauce can be prepared up to 3 days in advance. The tuna can be prepared up to 12 hours in advance and refrigerated. Bake and serve as directed.

note: Miso is a unique flavoring agent used prominently in Japanese cuisine. Shiro (or white) miso is a slightly sweet, light yellow soybean paste made with salt and malted rice. It is easily found in Japanese specialty markets, some supermarkets, and health-food stores.

note: Soak the bamboo skewers in water for at least fifteen minutes before using to prevent splintering and burning.

yield: ABOUT 36 SKEWERS

red, hot, and cool

CRISPY RADISHES WITH SEASONED-YOGURT DIPPING SAUCE

So light, so cool, so crisp, and soooooo simple, this hors d'oeuvre can't be beat during the summer months. Don't hesitate to whip up this Indian-inspired finger food the next time you entertain.

24 (about 3 bunches) small red radishes

$3/4$ cup plain whole-milk yogurt

$1/2$ cup finely chopped seeded cucumber

$1/4$ cup sour cream

$1/4$ cup finely chopped fresh mint

3 tablespoons finely chopped red onion

$1 1/2$ teaspoons seasoned rice vinegar

1 teaspoon fresh lime juice

$1/2$ teaspoon grated ginger

$1/2$ teaspoon kosher salt

Make 2 cuts in the shape of an **X**, from the root end to the center of each radish. Place in a bowl of ice water and refrigerate until the radishes open up, at least 1 hour. Strain.

Mix the yogurt, cucumber, sour cream, mint, onion, vinegar, lime juice, ginger, and kosher salt together in a medium bowl. Refrigerate until chilled. Serve with the radishes.

do-ahead tips: The radishes and the yogurt dip can be prepared up to 1 day in advance. (Do not add the cucumbers and mint to the yogurt until 3 hours before serving.)

yield: 24 RADISHES

light and delicate

leaves of glory

ARTICHOKE LEAVES WITH PARMESAN-BASIL AIOLI

When serving this hors d'oeuvre, don't forget to include an extra bowl or wineglass as a dispenser for the "already eaten" artichoke leaves. Serve these make-ahead morsels at any party and you will be able to kick back and rest on your laurels.

2 large artichokes	1 tablespoon lemon juice
$1/2$ lemon	$1/4$ teaspoon minced garlic
$3/4$ cup mayonnaise	$1/8$ teaspoon pepper
$1/3$ cup grated Parmesan cheese	2 tablespoons finely chopped fresh parsley for garnishing
3 tablespoons chopped fresh basil	

Trim the stems of the artichokes flush with the bottom of the leaves. Trim the tops 1 to $1^1/2$ inches. Remove 2 to 3 layers of the leaves around the bottoms and trim the remaining leaves with scissors to remove the thorns on the top. To prevent discoloration, rub all of the cut surfaces with the lemon. Cook in a steamer until tender and leaves can be pulled off easily, 45 minutes to 1 hour. Let cool.

Combine the mayonnaise, Parmesan, basil, lemon juice, garlic, and pepper in a small bowl. Refrigerate until chilled.

Gently remove the leaves from the artichoke, starting at the base, until the center is reached. Arrange the leaves flesh-side up on baking sheets. Remove and discard the small, thin center leaves. Using a spoon, scrape off the choke—the prickly, inedible center. Discard. Trim the heart with a knife to remove any tough areas. Finely chop the hearts and add to the mayonnaise mixture.

(continued)

light and delicate

to assemble: Place 1 teaspoon of the mayonnaise mixture on each artichoke leaf. (Make sure that each leaf is sturdy.) Arrange on a dish with the "handle" portion facing out and garnish with chopped parsley.

do-ahead tips: The artichokes can be cooked up to 2 days in advance, covered tightly, and refrigerated. The mayonnaise mixture can be prepared up to 3 days in advance and refrigerated. The filled leaves can be assembled up to 1 day in advance, covered with plastic wrap, and refrigerated.

yield: ABOUT 48 FILLED LEAVES

tofu teasers

CELERY STUFFED WITH CREAMY HERBED TOFU

We offered these salad boats at a bridal luncheon this past spring, knowing that the honoree was a vegetarian. She wasn't the only one who enjoyed these deceptively healthy treats.

8 ounces extra-firm tofu, patted dry

1/4 cup chopped fresh basil

1 tablespoon chopped fresh dill

1 tablespoon extra-virgin olive oil

1 tablespoon lemon juice

1/2 teaspoon minced garlic

4 teaspoons kosher salt

1/8 teaspoon pepper

4 medium celery stalks, trimmed

14 cups water

3 cups ice

24 fresh dill sprigs for garnishing

Combine the tofu, basil, dill, olive oil, lemon juice, garlic, 1/2 teaspoon of the kosher salt, and pepper in the food processor. Process until smooth and creamy. Refrigerate until chilled.

Peel a thin strip off the length of each celery stalk so that the stalks lay flat. Cut into 1-inch lengths on the diagonal. Mix 8 cups of the water and 2 teaspoons of the kosher salt in a medium saucepan. Bring to a boil. Add the celery and cook until the color brightens, about 1 minute. Mix the ice, remaining 6 cups water, and remaining 1 1/2 teaspoons kosher salt together in a large bowl. Plunge the celery into the ice water to stop the cooking process. Transfer the celery to a paper towel–lined plate and refrigerate.

to assemble: Spoon 1 teaspoon of the tofu mixture onto each piece of celery and garnish with a dill sprig.

do-ahead tips: The tofu mixture can be prepared up to 2 days in advance. The celery can be blanched up to 1 day in advance. Assemble up to 3 hours in advance and refrigerate until ready to serve.

yield: 24 FILLED CELERY PIECES

light and delicate

chive talkin' scallops

PARMESAN CRISPS WITH SCALLOPS AND CHIVES

There is no doubt about it, this hors d'oeuvre is truly spectacular. In order for the Parmesan crisps to turn out properly, they must be made with top-quality, freshly grated Parmesan cheese on a day with very little humidity. Ask your deli for freshly grated cheese and test it with one or two crisps before preparing this recipe. An acceptable substitute is bite-sized melba toast.

$1/4$ cup Parmesan cheese, finely grated (see recipe introduction)

12 small (about $1/2$ pound) sea scallops, trimmed to $3/4$-inch high

$1/8$ teaspoon kosher salt

$1/8$ teaspoon white pepper

4 tablespoons ($1/2$ stick) unsalted butter

White truffle oil (optional)

1 tablespoon finely chopped fresh chives for garnishing

Preheat the oven to 400°F.

Drop the Parmesan, 1 teaspoon at a time, $1^{1}/2$ inches apart, onto a foil-lined baking sheet. Lightly press each mound to create a circle the size of a quarter. Bake until crispy and light brown, 8 to 10 minutes. Let cool. Gently transfer to a baking sheet with a spatula and cover with plastic wrap until ready to assemble.

Season the scallops with the kosher salt and white pepper. Melt 2 tablespoons of the butter in a medium nonstick skillet over medium heat. Add half of the scallops and cook until barely cooked through, about 2 minutes per side. Transfer to a paper towel–lined baking sheet. Wipe out the skillet and return to the stove. Melt the remaining 2 tablespoons butter. Add the remaining scallops and cook until barely cooked through, about 2 minutes. Set with the other scallops.

to assemble: Top each crisp with a scallop. Drizzle with white truffle oil and garnish with chives. Serve immediately.

(continued)

do-ahead tips: The Parmesan crisps can be prepared up to 2 days in advance and stored in an airtight container at room temperature or frozen up to 1 week in advance. Thaw before assembling. The scallops can be slightly undercooked up to 8 hours in advance, refrigerated, and warmed in a 350°F oven for 3 to 5 minutes before assembly.

yield: 12 CRISPS

chix stix

LEMON CHICKEN AND SNOW PEAS ON SKEWERS

The lively combination of lemon, chicken, and crunchy snow peas revs up the palate. For a dramatic presentation, we like to serve these skewers on a glass platter covered entirely with paper-thin slices of lemon.

1¼ pounds boneless, skinless chicken breasts, cut into ¾-inch cubes

½ cup plus 3 tablespoons fresh lemon juice

3 tablespoons brown sugar

2 tablespoons water

1 tablespoon plus 1 teaspoon grated lemon zest

1½ teaspoons kosher salt

½ cup all-purpose flour

1 teaspoon paprika

¼ teaspoon pepper

6 tablespoons vegetable oil

36 snow peas, cut into 1-inch diagonal pieces, blanched

36 five-inch bamboo skewers (see Note)

Pour 3 tablespoons of the lemon juice over the chicken and toss to coat in a medium bowl. Let marinate for at least 30 minutes.

Combine the remaining ½ cup lemon juice, brown sugar, water, lemon zest, and ½ teaspoon of the kosher salt in a medium bowl.

Drain the chicken and pat dry with paper towels. Put the flour, remaining 1 teaspoon kosher salt, paprika, and pepper in a plastic bag and shake to mix well. Add the chicken and shake to coat the chicken completely.

Heat 3 tablespoons of the vegetable oil in a large nonstick skillet over high heat. Add half the chicken and cook until crispy and brown on all sides, about 4 minutes. Transfer to a paper towel–lined baking sheet using a slotted spoon. Wipe out the skillet and return to the stove. Add the remaining 3 tablespoons vegetable oil. Add the remaining chicken

(continued)

light and delicate

113

and cook until crispy and brown on all sides, about 4 minutes. Transfer to a paper towel–lined baking sheet using a slotted spoon.

Add the chicken to the lemon juice mixture and toss to coat well. Pour into a 14-by-9-by-2-inch glass baking dish. Refrigerate 8 hours or overnight.

to assemble: Preheat the oven to 350°F. Slide 1 piece of snow pea onto a skewer followed by 1 piece of chicken and another piece of snow pea. Repeat until all of the ingredients have been used. Cover in foil and bake until warm, about 5 minutes. Or serve slightly chilled.

do-ahead tips: The chicken can be prepared up to 1 day in advance. The skewers can be assembled up to 8 hours in advance and refrigerated. Bake as directed or remove from the refrigerator and let sit 20 minutes before serving.

note: Soak the bamboo skewers in water for at least fifteen minutes before using to prevent splintering and burning.

yield: 36 SKEWERS

shrimply delish

POACHED SHRIMP WITH CILANTRO AND SWEET 'N' SOUR GLAZE

This dish is a contemporary version of the long-revered shrimp cocktail. The glaze is a modern blend of spicy and tangy flavors with an Asian accent. Don't forget to set out a small bowl for the shrimp tails.

GLAZE:

1/3 cup plus 1 tablespoon water

1/4 cup seasoned rice vinegar (see Note)

2 teaspoons finely chopped lemongrass, inner white bulb only

2 teaspoons minced peeled fresh ginger

1 teaspoon lime zest

1/4 teaspoon crushed red pepper

1 1/2 teaspoons cornstarch

12 cups water

1 tablespoon kosher salt

24 medium to large shrimp

24 fresh cilantro leaves for garnishing

Combine 1/3 cup of the water, vinegar, lemongrass, ginger, lime zest, and crushed red pepper in a small nonreactive saucepan. Dissolve the cornstarch in 1 tablespoon water in a small bowl and add to the vinegar mixture using a whisk. Bring to a boil over medium heat, whisking at least twice. Boil for 1 minute. Transfer to a bowl and refrigerate until chilled.

Bring the remaining 12 cups of water and kosher salt to a boil in a large saucepan over medium heat. Add the shrimp and cook until opaque in the center, about 3 minutes. Strain. Arrange on a baking sheet with a lip. Refrigerate until partially chilled.

to assemble: Peel the shrimp, leaving the tail attached. Cut a slit (1/2 to 3/4 inch deep) down the back of each shrimp from the top to the tail. Be careful not to cut completely through the shrimp. Rinse the shrimp in a bowl of cold water to remove the vein. Transfer to a paper towel–lined plate to absorb any excess water. Place a cilantro sprig in the cut of each shrimp. Brush with the glaze before serving.

(continued)

light and delicate

do-ahead tips: The glaze can be prepared up to 3 days in advance. The shrimp can be assembled up to 1 day in advance (without the glaze) and refrigerated. Serve as directed.

note: If you cannot find seasoned rice vinegar, add 1 tablespoon sugar and $^3/_4$ teaspoon kosher salt to $^1/_4$ cup unseasoned rice vinegar as a substitute.

yield: 24 SHRIMP

rosemary's tartlets

MINIATURE TARTLETS FILLED WITH WALNUTS,

BRIE, AND GRAPE SALSA

The secret to success with this recipe is to seek out a high-quality Brie. We prefer imported French Brie to domestic varieties. When you purchase Brie, it should have a soft consistency without being runny. Once a wheel of Brie is cut, it will not ripen further, so if you purchase an under-ripe portion, it will stay that way.

1 cup seedless red grapes, cut in half

$1/4$ teaspoon kosher salt

2 tablespoons finely chopped green onion, green part only

1 tablespoon balsamic vinegar

2 teaspoons walnut oil (see Note, page 57)

$1/4$ teaspoon chopped fresh rosemary

$1/4$ teaspoon minced garlic

$1/8$ teaspoon pepper

Forty-eight $1 1/2$-inch-round savory pastry shells (see Note)

$1/2$ cup walnuts, toasted and chopped

8 ounces Brie, rind removed

light and delicate

Preheat the oven to 300°F.

Put the grapes and kosher salt in a food processor and pulse until the grapes are coarsely chopped. Transfer to a strainer; let sit for at least 10 minutes. Mix the green onion, vinegar, oil, rosemary, garlic, and pepper together in a small bowl. Add the grapes and mix well.

to assemble: Arrange the shells on a baking sheet and fill each with $1/2$ teaspoon walnuts, $1/2$ teaspoon Brie, and $1/2$ teaspoon grape salsa (use a fork to transfer the salsa to the shells to avoid capturing too much liquid). Bake until the cheese begins to melt, about 5 minutes; do not overbake. Serve immediately.

do-ahead tips: The grape salsa can be prepared up to 1 day in advance and refrigerated (do not add the walnut oil until ready to assemble). The tarts can be partially assembled with the walnuts and Brie up to 6 hours in advance. Add the salsa up to 30 minutes in advance. Bake as directed.

note: Our favorite brand of pre-made tartlet shells is made by Albert Uster Imports, Inc. Call them at 800-231-8154 and order item number L90400. The minimum order is 432, but don't be alarmed. They last for up to one year and they can be filled with a myriad of ingredients, making them very convenient to have on hand for impromptu parties. You may even want to split an order with a friend.

yield: 48 TARTLETS

light and delicate

goat-teas

OPEN-FACED GOAT CHEESE, CUCUMBER, AND
PICKLED RED ONION TEA SANDWICHES

This hors d'oeuvre is particularly good with buttermilk bread because of its soft texture. The robust cheese and tangy onions complement the crisp cucumbers. They are ideal for a daytime party.

3/4 cup seasoned rice vinegar (see Note, page 118)

2 cups thinly sliced red onion (cut the onion in half lengthwise, then place flat-side down, cut off the top and peel, then slice from the top to the stem)

2/3 cup goat cheese, at room temperature

1/3 cup cream cheese, at room temperature

1/8 teaspoon white pepper

12 slices white bread, crusts removed, cut into 3-inch squares

1 English cucumber, cut into 1/16-inch slices, cut in half

Pour the vinegar over the onions and let marinate in a small bowl until the onions are soft and malleable, at least 30 minutes. Strain and refrigerate until chilled.

Mix the goat cheese and cream cheese together in a small bowl. Season with the white pepper.

to assemble: Spread about 1 tablespoon of the cheese mixture on each piece of bread. Cut each piece of bread into 4 triangles. Arrange 3 half slices of the cucumber on each triangle. Top with 2 to 3 slices of the marinated onion.

do-ahead tips: The cheese mixture can be prepared up to 3 days in advance and refrigerated. Return to room temperature before using. The sandwiches can be assembled up to 2 hours in advance, covered with plastic wrap, and left at room temperature until ready to serve.

yield: 48 SANDWICHES

light and delicate

cocktail recipes

classic martini

The martini never goes out of style, as it is the cornerstone of cocktail culture. The simplicity of this powerful drink makes it all the more enticing to prepare.

8 ounces gin or vodka

Whisper of vermouth

Pour the gin or vodka into a shaker filled with ice. Add the vermouth. Cover and shake. Drain the martini mixture into chilled glasses and garnish with olives or a lemon twist.

SERVES 4

jala-tini

If you want to spice up your martinis, consider serving this Cajun-inspired version. Garnish the glass with a jalapeño pepper.

8 ounces vodka

1 tablespoon coarsely chopped jalapeño, seeded

2 teaspoons lemon zest

$1/4$ teaspoon coarsely chopped garlic

Combine the vodka, jalapeño, lemon zest, and garlic in a glass jar with a lid. Cover and let sit at room temperature until the vodka absorbs the flavors of the other ingredients, at least 24 hours and up to 72 hours. Strain the vodka into colorful glasses filled with ice.

SERVES 4

world-class margarita

It would take thorough searching to find someone who doesn't love a good margarita. This recipe is a traditional blend of tequila and lime and is so versatile that it should be part of everyone's cocktail repertoire.

4 ounces gold tequila

4 ounces triple sec

4 ounces fresh lime juice

$1/4$ cup plus 1 tablespoon superfine sugar

Coarse salt for lining the rims of the glasses

4 lime wheels for garnishing

Rub the rim of each glass with a lime wheel. Place the salt in a small saucer and dip the glasses into it. Pour the tequila, triple sec, lime juice, and sugar into a shaker filled with ice. Cover and shake well. Strain the margarita mixture into the prepared glasses and garnish with the lime wheels.

SERVES 4

frozen peach-a-rita

This intensely fruity margarita is a fun alternative to the traditional version. For a large crowd, try making several batches ahead of time and storing them in the freezer. Let the frozen mixture sit at room temperature until it reaches the desired consistency.

4 cups chopped frozen peaches

1 cup orange juice

4 large ice cubes

4 ounces tequila

4 ounces peach schnapps

1 tablespoon fresh lime juice

1 teaspoon grenadine

4 fresh peach slices or lime wheels for garnish

Place the peaches, orange juice, ice cubes, tequila, peach schnapps, lime juice, and grenadine in the blender. Blend until smooth. Pour into large margarita glasses or 10-ounce wineglasses. Garnish with peach slices or lime wheels.

SERVES 4

traditional kir royale

No wonder this concoction of cassis and champagne has stood the test of time. The cassis adds an extra touch of sweetness to the classic bubbly that we know and love.

One 750-milliliter bottle of champagne or sparkling wine

2 ounces cassis

Fresh raspberries for garnish

Pour 5 ounces of champagne into 4 flutes. Pour $1/2$ ounce of cassis into each glass. Garnish with a few raspberries and serve. Seal the champagne bottle with a stopper or insert a silver spoon into the neck to maintain the carbonation, and refrigerate for later.

SERVES 4

apricot sparkler

This aperitif is inspired by one that we drank at Chateau d'Esclimont, outside of Paris. It was so delicious that we made our own version upon our return to the U.S. We still drink this combination of flavors on festive occasions.

16 ounces champagne or
    sparkling wine

4 ounces apricot nectar

Brandy

4 sugar cubes

Pour 4 ounces of champagne into 4 flutes. Add 1 ounce of apricot nectar and a splash of brandy to each flute. Drop 1 sugar cube into each drink and serve.

SERVES 4

index

table of equivalents

THE EXACT EQUIVALENTS IN THE FOLLOWING TABLES
HAVE BEEN ROUNDED FOR CONVENIENCE.

Liquid/Dry Measures

U.S.	METRIC
¼ teaspoon	1.25 milliliters
½ teaspoon	2.5 milliliters
1 teaspoon	5 milliliters
1 tablespoon (3 teaspoons)	
	15 milliliters
1 fluid ounce (2 tablespoons)	
	30 milliliters
¼ cup	60 milliliters
⅓ cup	80 milliliters
½ cup	120 milliliters
1 cup	240 milliliters
1 pint (2 cups)	480 milliliters
1 quart (4 cups, 32 ounces)	
	960 milliliters
1 gallon (4 quarts)	3.84 liters
1 ounce (by weight)	28 grams
1 pound	454 grams
2.2 pounds	1 kilogram

Length

U.S.	METRIC
⅛ inch	3 millimeters
¼ inch	6 millimeters
½ inch	12 millimeters
1 inch	2.5 centimeters

Oven Temperature

FAHRENHEIT	CELSIUS	GAS
250	120	½
275	140	1
300	150	2
325	160	3
350	180	4
375	190	5
400	200	6
425	220	7
450	230	8
475	240	9
500	260	10

Photographer's acknowledgments

Crate & Barrel: stemware/barware throughout; Cyclamen (Emeryville, CA): 24; Dransfield & Ross: 38; Dupuis (Del Mar, CA/Scottsdale, AZ): 98, 102; Feast (Pasadena): 32; The Folk Tree Collection (Pasadena): 18, 62; Freehand (Los Angeles): 73, 84; Ann Gish Studios (Newbury Park, CA): 122; Joel, Inc. (Spokane): 56, 100; Magpie (Manhattan Beach, CA): 32, 68; Niki Stix (Novato, CA): 100; Noteworthy (Los Angeles): 120; Olivers (Pasadena): 76; Quari (Manhattan Beach, CA): 120; Rusty Nail (Ventura, CA): 76, 90; Salutations (Beverly Hills): 106; San Marino Hardware (San Marino, CA): 120; Tesoro (Beverly Hills): 73, 76, 81, 102; Translations (Dallas): 106; Wally's (Los Angeles): wine/spirits throughout; Alison Wright Architects (Los Angeles), location courtesy of: 81; The Woods (Brentwood, CA): 98; Zipper (Los Angeles): cover, 46, 84.